Tracy —

Happy cooking!

— Les

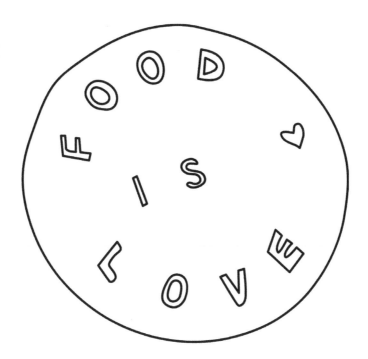

Leslie Hart-Davidson

HDD Studios
559 E. Sherwood Road
Williamston, MI 48895
www.hddbook.com

Orders by U.S. trade bookstores and wholesalers.
Please contact Distribution: Tel: (517) 889-5071 or visit www.hddbook.com.

Printed in the United States of America

First Printing, 2021

ISBN 978-0991636037
No unicorns were harmed in the making of this book. Some names and identifying details have been changed to protect the privacy of individuals.

Cover Design & Illustration Copyright © 2021 by Amber Telman
Book design and production by Sara Reedy
Interior illustrations © 2016 Molly Gates & © 2021 Amber Telman
Photography Leslie Hart-Davidson, except the pie picture, Bill Hart-Davidson took that gem.

Kitten: Ppprrrpppppprrrrrrrrrpppppppmeowwwwwwwwwwwwwwwwwww!
Third time's a charm. Thank you again for putting up with me and inspiring me to produce even more content. I'll never tire of your big, beautiful brain and your giant, kind heart.

Becca and Rachel: I'm so, so grateful to have you both in my orbit. I'd like to think I'm the mentor, but I'm positive you've taught me much, much more than I've been able to teach you. I love and respect you both. There's no place like evil lair.

BHD: Thanks for sharing your family and your love of cooking with me. I'll try my best not to apple-chimi-cheesecake up any more of your meals.

Mike Mike Mike: May the force be with you. Thank you for always making me see the light.

Jim Hart: Dad, you'd love this book and the lessons and the humanity and the Jim-isms. Good talk.

Mary Hart: Mom, will we be having any delicious side dishes with our frozen waffles? No? Ok. Screw you guys! I'm going home!

JJ: Let's finish the bottle and call it a day. Here's what you SHOULD do (point point point.) Can we have pannnnncakes? One tug and it's done! Hey, that's mine! Let's file that appropriately. I don't use ketchup! Might as well. Where's my money, bitch? Ken Starr said WHAT? Jesus Christ CAT! Just do what Jen says. Are you ok with that trip? Fuck COVID! Sigh...cookie.

Lillian: Good goddess, maybe one day you'll eat what I cook. Karma's a bitch, kid. I love you to the moon and back anyway. Wait, I love you the most. Ha! Superlatives!

Greg: It was an honor to be your little sister (except when you crashed my Big Wheel), to care for you, and to feed you. You would have loved the Compound. Thank you for the opportunity to be a better human. I'm trying reallllllllllly hard.

Spice & Boutros: All the gratitude. All of it. We'll always have each other (and summer vacations. And raunchy texting. Annnnd a mutual disdain for smarmy smooth jazz.)

Patti Bills: You are everything that is good and kind in this world and I love you to bits.

for greg.

Hey there, reader! Before you dive into the book, heads up: this isn't a traditional cookbook. Here's an instruction manual for properly navigating Food is Love. Enjoy!

If your goal is to **FEED YOUR BELLY**
Recipes are sprinkled throughout the book in each section following the Brotatochip saga and its accompanying lessons. You'll find a hella-useful index of all main dishes, appetizers, desserts and party fare on page 306.

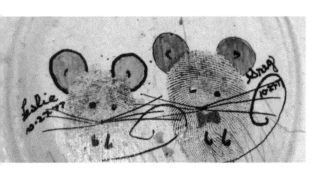

If your goal is to **FEED YOUR SOUL**
The five Brotatochip stories begin each section and tell the tale of how I took care of my big brother Greg during his brave fight with cancer. The first three sections also contain self-help content through stories of how cooking makes us better humans.

If your goal is to **FEED YOUR BRAIN**
Kitchen design using the principles of CRAP and TALC and the history of kitchens are prominently featured in section four to help you better understand what makes a beautiful, functional space to practice Food is Love.

clear list of needed
ingredients over here

fun antecdote about
the who and why for
each recipe

stunning pictures of
delicious noms - wipe
off the drool and start
cooking

prosciutto-bound asparagus
your pee is gonna smell sooooo funny

M y pal Mike introduced me to the joy of wrapping things with porktastic goodness years ago. Melon, corn on the cob, and various veggies just minding their own business being healthy and stuff were suddenly transformed into glorious bites of salty, fatty heaven.

Asparagus is a perfect recipient of the prosciutto treatment because of its similar cooking time. 30ish minutes in the oven at high heat yields a crisp porky wrap around perfectly al dente asparagus spears. Serve with yellow rice.

1 bunch fresh asparagus spears
(about #2 pencil diameter)
1 package prosciutto (about 5oz)
3 T evoo
Salt and pepper to taste

Preheat the oven to 425 degrees. Rinse the asparagus carefully and cut the woody bottoms off to a uniform length. Take each prosciutto slice and carefully tear it apart lengthwise to make 2 strips. Starting at the tip, wrap the prosciutto strip snugly around the asparagus stalk. Continue until the strips run out.

Place the wrapped stalks in a pyrex baking dish and surround them with any remaining naked stalks. Drizzle the evoo over the asparagus and shimmy the dish to ensure the oil is evenly distributed and the stalks won't stick.

Bake for 30ish minutes until the asparagus spears are fork-tender. Serve over a bed of rice.

Serves: 4
Pairs with: a sharp knife and a big glass of water.
Consideration: easy bougie meal to impress guests.

54
Food is Love

55

A drizzle of balsamic glaze tastes amazeballs.

clear instructions found
right over here - if they
are not clear enough,
find me on social media
@hddstudiosofficial,
i'll hook you up

survey information
to check out before
you begin

pro-tips and cheat
codes to up your
skills game

Leslie Hart-Davidson

Welcome to Food is Love, a manifesto of emotions through the act of cooking. Come for the food, stay for the self-help, and leave with your belly and heart full.

You probably picked up this cookbook with the intention of looking at new recipes to inspire you or guilt you into cooking or make you think "I'll never, ever in a million years be able to make that." It's cool. No matter what the reason, you're still in the right place. Consider me your tour guide on an adventure of food that will lead you to unexpected places.

My name is Leslie Hart-Davidson. I'm a residential interior designer by trade and have written two other home-related books. *Remodeling Your House without Killing Your Spouse* was my first, followed by *It's Not Your Room, it's You*. I wrote both with the intention of helping folks live better in their homes though great interior design advice and a healthy serving of self-reflection.

My goal for *Food is Love* is similar: to help cooks express their love for family, friends and community through food. Think of this book as a mashup of researcher/storyteller/general badass Brené Brown, and my hero/culinary genius/foodie educator Alton Brown. This pairing of brilliant Browns is the perfect way for me to explain both my love and motivation for cooking.

During a SxSW conference speech about courage, Brené said this: "The brokenhearted are the bravest among us because they have the courage to love." I'd consider it courageous to write a cookbook that could rightfully be shelved in the self-help section. As you read through the main story of how I cared for my big brother Greg during his six-month battle with cancer, you'll understand how I channeled my broken heart into cooking for others.

Before you think "Oh great, this will be a depressing-ass cookbook," please keep in mind that I'm more Chrissy Teigen than Debbie Downer. The recipes and stories throughout the book will be filled with plenty of foul language and comic relief. I pinky swear you'll enjoy reading it.

I'd consider it courageous to write a cookbook that could rightfully be shelved in the self-help section.

Much of my inspiration to become a better-educated cook came from Alton Brown. Watching so many years of *Good Eats* on the Food Network not only encouraged me to level up my foodie game, but also to share those new skills with friends and family. "We're all so busy taking Facebook pictures of our food, we never take pictures of the people sitting across from us... We've shifted away from the things that actually matter in human interaction," Alton said.

Outside of the touchy/feely/cooky realm, *Food is Love* has some terrific practical applications. I wasn't about to let my design background go to waste, so you'll enjoy a chapter about kitchen design and layout features. The CRAP and TALC chapters are reinventions of the acronyms used in my first two design books with the bonus of helping you create and hone a space where you'll actually *like* to cook.

Please keep one thing in mind if you're looking at the photos of dishes in Food is Love thinking that they're unattainable and you can never cook like that: **I am not a chef.** Take comfort in the idea that a regular person who farts around in the kitchen can whip up some tasty things for others. I may be a professionally trained and credentialed interior designer, but I'm a provincially trained cook. You are just as capable as I am of making every damn dish in this cookbook, and my mission is to make you give a shit about feeding people. No matter what your level of skill or how much effort you want to put into meal prep, Food is Love.

Leslie Hart-Davidson

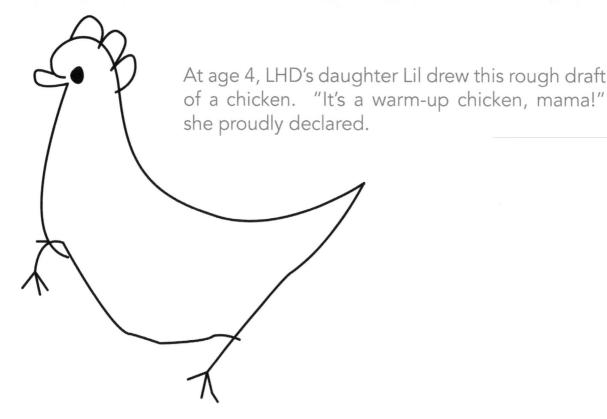

At age 4, LHD's daughter Lil drew this rough draft of a chicken. "It's a warm-up chicken, mama!" she proudly declared.

Contributor Credit

Many thanks to these special people who made *Food is Love* possible with their generous donations!

Jennifer Corbett • Sarah Anway • Jenn Stewart • Donna Donovan • Chris Soden • Michael O'Connell • Ben Lauren
Megan Dunson • Christine Withers • Michele Simmons • Brian Kimmel • Tracy Popey • Jason Reed • Liza Potts
Erin & Tim Amidon • Who's Sara? • Joshua Edwards • Lydia Wilkes • Katie Mihalarogiannis • Pat Everett • Jeff Chambers
Sam Edwards • Tammy Conard-Salvo • Derek G. Ross • Allegra Smith • Wilbur Massie • Suzie Rumsey • Chris Copeland
Alyssa Puryear (bark!) • Lil' Meiring • Beth Keller Kirycki • Lori Lyn Peterson • Antoinette Grace Hui • Matt Cutter
Leah Near • Rebecca Rickley • Cindy Mello • Mike McLeod • Shiron Musick • Bill & Erica WIlliamson • Phil Deaton
Teresa Mangum • Peter Rees • Audrey Swartz • Squeaky • Scott Pennington & Purdom Lindblad • Mitch Runge & Eugene Yi
Steve Amidon • Steve & Annette • Tim Krause • Karen Bastien • Geoffrey Clegg • Heather Galecka • Victor Meng
Rachel Pavlik • Mel & Richie • Major Lee Kimmel • Trixie Long Smith • Nicole Gudeman • Sharon Pastuszka • Patti Bills
Kirk Montgomery • Michelle Eble • Kami Marie • Kellie Meyer • Terry and Cathy Watson • Anita Duenas • Stuart Selber
Joanie Mills • Amiee Dragon (meow!) • Sue McLeod • Suzie and Bruce Van Hal • Jim Ridolfo • Donnie Johnson Sackey
Robin Fisher • Sean Davidson • Jessie Moore • David Williamson • Mollie Hearns • Judy Kimmel

Pandemic Foreward

Shit got weird in 2020. The majority of this cookbook was written prior to the Pandemic when my validation for being a good human and motivation to help others came directly from cooking nightly dinners for family, lunches for HDD Studios interns, and fabulous cuisine for friends during weekly dinner parties. Having to socially distance during in 2020 really fucked with my identity and purpose. I feed people. It's what I do.

To maintain my sanity, I had to develop a new normal when it became apparent in early summer 2020 that social distancing would be a thing until well after a vaccine was invented and distributed in 2021. The new normal became weekly Zoom dinners with friends where we tandem cooked the same recipe and dined together with our laptop as a guest at the table. It also became joining our foodie friends' Facebook community of pizza lovers to post submission pics of our interpretation of the week's rotating pizza theme assignment. Lastly, the new normal became taking meals to friends who were Covid-positive and sending grocery deliveries to families short on cash from the Pandemic stresses.

My dining room is empty for now, but my heart is full of love for those I look forward to feeding. We'll get through this eventually if we all just give.

When in doubt, give more.

Leslie Hart-Davidson

The Emergency

In September of 2017, my big brother Greg, age 50, collapsed in his kitchen. Greg was a handsome devil and led a healthy lifestyle, working a physically demanding job as a merchandiser for Pepsi and constantly honing his ripped physique by lifting weights. He lived alone but had close friends and many female admirers. They had all noticed that he seemed a bit hoarse for the summer months, but Greg easily passed it off as allergies.

When Greg texted me from Ohio on September 19th, he told me that he had passed out and thought he broke his nose. "I worked 50 hours this week but haven't been eating the last few days. I think I'm just dehydrated," he explained. "I'll go to Urgent Care and have them give me a bag of saline. I'm sure I'll be back to work tomorrow."

I read the text while sitting in my design studio in Michigan. I showed Greg's message to my business manager Jen, who looked concerned. "My spidey senses are telling me that you need to get in the car RIGHT NOW and go to him. Throw your shit in a bag and go right now. Do it."

I arrived at the emergency room at 9pm. Greg had tried to get treatment at the Urgent Care facility, but they sent him directly to the ER. I found him on a gurney in a tiny curtained room looking grim. "Cancer," he whispered, his voice so hoarse I had to lean close to hear. "They did an Xray and found a giant mass in my throat. That's why I can't talk and have been waking up at night with my neck hurting. The surgeon will come tomorrow morning and look at what's happening." I stared at him, stunned.

Food is Love

"I'm glad you're here," he said to me. "I didn't want to be alone."

My brother and I had lost our parents years before and only had each other. He was unmarried and lived alone. "You're not alone now," I told him. "I'll see you through this. I promise."

The next morning, Greg had more tests to determine the course of care for his mass. A kind thoracic surgeon came in to talk to me before Greg returned from tests. "We need to do emergency surgery. Your brother has thyroid cancer. The mass has been growing for years and has eaten through his esophagus. Everything your brother has eaten or drunk the last month has fallen into his chest cavity. We'll need to remove his esophagus and bypass with a feeding tube. He's weak, only 102lbs on his 5'9" frame, so I'm not sure he'll survive the surgery."

Greg looked surprisingly calm when I saw him right before the surgery. "Hey," he said. The doctor explained in detail what he would be doing to Greg over the next 4-6 hours. "Do you have any questions?" the doctor asked my brother. Greg looked at him with great concern and said this: "Can you keep me alive until December 15th when Star Wars comes out?"

The entire medical staff erupted in laughter. "YES!" the doctor replied. "I'm pretty sure we can make that happen for you!"

Can you keep me alive until December 15th, when Star Wars comes out?

Greg looked at me when the staff had left. He gave me specific instructions if he didn't survive the surgery. "I love you to death," he said.

15

Leslie Hart-Davidson

I spent the early hours of the surgery visiting my mama's grave and asking her a million questions. I stared at her little niche across from the fountain and sobbed. Twenty-four hours before, I was oblivious to my brother's condition. Now, I was pleading with my mama to keep him alive. "February," I heard her voice say in my head. Five months. Just five months to help my only brother. I prepared myself to Give in a way I had never given before.

Eight hours later, the nurse came to get me as I sat with friends and a few extended family members outside the ICU. She held out her hand and said "let's go." I joined her for the long walk to my brother's room. "Honey, he coded." she said as soon as we were away from the other folks. As I contorted my face in anguish, she quickly said "We got him back, but it's touchy. You need to talk to him right away and tell him to stay."

The nurse deposited me in the throng of a dozen medical professionals who were surrounding Greg, poking and prodding at all the wires and tubes coming from his body. "Go to him," she said. I approached the cyborg that was impersonating my brother and looked for a place to touch him that wouldn't hurt or displace the spaghetti-like wires. I settled my hand on his head and watched as the ventilator breathed for him. I pushed the long hair off his regal, unwrinkled forehead, bending down to his ear so he could hear me. The eyes of all the staff were on me, ready to hear the sweet things I would stay to convince my brother to stay on this earthy plane. "DON'T EVER FUCKING SCARE ME LIKE THAT AGAIN," I said. The medical team roared with laughter. Greg's lips curled in a smile around his vent tube. He didn't open his eyes, but I knew he could hear me. "Mom can't have you yet," I said. "You have to stay with me." He nodded.

Food is Love

badass, big brother Greg

Jim Hart with baby Greg

Follow my brother's journey in each new *Food is Love* Chapter, told through these Brotato Chip stories.

17

barbie saves the day

"Oh nooooo!" Greg yelled deviously as he tossed another one of my baby dolls down the newly constructed laundry chute. At age 5, I resented my big brother's antics and would cry each time he misused my Dad's super cool bathroom creation for anything other than towels or clothes. Teary-eyed, I descended the stairs to find Baby Alive or Holly Hobbie splayed on top of the dryer awaiting retrieval. They looked at me expectantly as I took them back to my room for another tea party, daring me to fight back.

At age 7, I graduated to Barbies instead of baby dolls. Greg and his buddies gleefully tossed those down the laundry chute as well but quickly tired of my yelling and left to play Star Wars in the garage instead. Their absence allowed me to raid Greg's room for his action figures. I rounded up G.I. Joe and as many plastic army men as my seersucker smock would allow, then headed to the laundry chute.

I played out an entire narrative where the little plastic army men marched in attack formation toward the enemy chute. One by one, I pushed them into the chute, replicating all the screams and explosion noises I had heard my brother and his friends use. The bigger G.I. Joe charged in bravely to fight the chute, but plummeted into the abyss along with his team. I leaned my head over the opening and heard them all calling for help on top of the dryer in the basement. G.I. Joe was splayed on top of the heap, staring at me with pleading, beady little eyes.

"Sit tight, Joe!" I yelled into the chasm. "Help is on the wayyyy!" Dashing into my room, I grabbed Barbie and returned to the scene. Barbie peered over the edge and addressed the fallen crew somberly. "Looks like you boys need a little help, huh?" Barbie asked. "Save us! Please!" the little mine sweeping solider said. "Hurry!" yelled the tiny bayonet dude. "Joe is crushing me!" the doggy-crawling figure grunted. Joe looked into Barbie's eyes, stretching out his molded plastic hand with a sad grimace.

I turned to Barbie and told her the plan. "I'll lower you down and you fetch the boys, mmmkay?" "Piece of cake!" Barbie responded. "But I need a way to repel!" I snatched my latest craft — a God's Eye fashioned from Popsicle sticks and yarn — and unwound a decent length for the rescue. Securing the yarn around Barbie's waist, I wished her luck as I bent her arm at a hella-awkward angle to assist in the recovery. Barbie cheered me on as I lowered the yarn into the belly of the beast. Carefully hovering her above the stack of fallen soldiers, I angled Barbie's mangled arm beneath Joe's armpit to secure a decent grip and began the slow ascent to the top of the chute. I watched as Barbie's smiling, cheerful face came into focus with a constipated-looking G.I. Joe balancing precariously below her. I snatched them both and celebrated with a dance party in the tiny bathroom. "Woohoooo! Barbie saves the day!" I yelled at them both. "Girls ROCK!!!"

Barbie quickly reminded me that she still needed to rescue the remaining little army dudes. "My arm won't hook them all, though," she explained as I began lowering her down again. Barbie and I were able to snag the soldiers who had a molded triangle formation, but the poor dudes with flat configurations were SOL. "Don't leave us here!" they pleaded as they watched their buddies rise up to safety. "Everyone is going home today, boys," Barbie promised. "It's a sticky situation, but I'll get you out of here!"

Inspired by Barbie's comment, I ran to the kitchen to find the masking tape. I wrapped a big wad around Barbie's chest below her boobs and lowered her again. I apologized to her as I splatted her on top of the remaining soldiers to stick them tight enough for the ride home. Three tape splats later, Barbie returned with the last tiny solider. I lined up the whole platoon on the bathroom counter with G.I. Joe standing in front. "Barbie," Joe began, "On behalf of all my men, I want to thank you for your brave rescue after the Battle of Chute. We'd like to present you with this gold star sticker for your bravery." Barbie stared cheer-

fully at Joe as he shoved the massive sticker over the last masking tape glob covering her boobs. "Sure thing, boys!" Barbie replied. "But next time, how about you make it a challenge for me?"

Barbie turned and winked at me. We returned all of the army men and G.I. Joe to Greg's bedroom and spent the rest of the afternoon repairing the God's Eye.

Greg fell in the laundry chute last September. It wasn't because he had been a typical older brother joking around; it was because life had pushed him head first into that chute through a series of ridiculous, unfortunate, head-shaking medical circumstances. Since then, I've been wrapping that yarn around my waist, bending my arm at awkward angles and trying with all my cheerful badass Barbie might to pull him out. Hold tight, Greg. Help is on the way.

you could just love him

In my last two books *Remodeling Your House without Killing Your Spouse* and *It's Not Your Room, it's You*, I've written many anecdotes about my parents and what a tremendous influence their lives and deaths made on my awareness of home improvement and being a decent human being. I'll round out the trifecta of parental lessons in this book by talking about another significant influence: food. I'd like to start by telling the story of how I learned from my dad that food can be an ultimate expression of love and acceptance.

In 1987 when I was a freshman in high school, my folks decided to divorce after 20+years of marriage. For financial reasons, they had to remain in the same home for THREE MORE YEARS together before the divorce could be finalized and the home could be sold. Those years were filled with angst, yelling, heartache, and a constant display of contentious behavior. Being a dutiful daughter to my mom, I quickly learned to always take her side of the story and was rewarded when I pointed out my dad's shortcomings to her. (In hindsight, I realize how shitty that was, but hey, I was 14 and desperately wanted my mom's approval.)

My mom and brother and I moved to a little rental a week before Christmas my senior year of high school after the divorce was finalized. I saw very little of my dad over the next year as I graduated and left for college. While he was always supportive emotionally and quite excited for my new adventures in school, I continued to be an asshole to him out of maternal obligation. (Again, super shitty.)

Food is Love

The summer after my first year in college, my fiancé Bill and I commuted 6 days a week to our jobs at King's Island amusement park. During the hour-long drive, I was frequently quite vocal about my dad's shortcomings. After a particularly long-winded rant about why my mom was pissed at dad again, Bill was quiet. He glanced over at me, then back at the road. "You know," he began, "You could just love him." He glanced at me, then continued when he saw the shocked expression on my face. "You spend so much energy being angry at him for his relationship with your mom, but you're an adult now and can have your own relationship with him. Just love him. Let everything else go and just love."

Those sentences turned my world completely upside down. The revelations hit me like a ton of bricks: I was a grown-ass woman. I didn't have to think what my mom thought. I could have my own relationship with my dad. I could have my dad in my life again. I was a complete and total asshole for how I had been treating him.

To this day, I point to that moment in time when Bill suggested the "just love him" idea as the greatest gift he's given me in our 30 years together. Bill created the opportunity for "dad 2.0" by helping me understand that I could build a new and improved relationship as an adult with my dad. It was a slow process, but each time I reached out to dad, he was absolutely delighted to respond and connect. You know the best way we connected regularly? You guessed it: FOOD. Each time I came home from college to visit, he'd offer to cook for me. Bill and my brother and I would visit him and eat ridiculously good food that he prepared with much anticipation, fanfare and love. My most frequently requested meal was meatballs and sauce prepared in the Rival avocado green 1970's crockpot that he would make in the morning and let simmer all day. The meatballs were mixed and browned first, then nestled gently in the bubbling sauce for up to 10 hours. It's a labor-inten-

21

sive meal, so I knew that asking dad to make the dish when he worked so many hours was a chore. He made it gladly each time I asked, though, because food is love.

In 2005 when dad passed away from a hard-fought battle with esophageal cancer, my brother Greg asked me what possessions I wanted from his house. "I'm guessing the crockpot?" he asked me. "Yup. And the ladle that he used to serve the sauce, please." I can't count the number of times I made meatballs and sauce in dad's crockpot. After mom died, I started making my brother meatballs and freezing them to take to Ohio as a special treat. Greg was a challenging person to buy gifts for since he wanted for very little, so cooking became a great gift option. I think dad would be pleased that his crockpot continued the food is love legacy after he passed.

I didn't fully realize how much attachment I had to that Rival avocado green 1970's crockpot until it met its demise. In 2016, Bill and our daughter took a day trip to Ohio to fetch a tiny kitten that my niece had rescued. I had promised Bill that I'd make meatballs and sauce to have when they returned that evening after the long trip. I browned the meatballs and prepared the sauce after they left, thinking happy thoughts about my dad and the great meals we had together after Bill had encouraged me with the "just love him" talk. My spidey senses were tingling a bit as they do when I feel dad hovering, but I dismissed it as just a happy remembrance. I had planned to run errands after I started the crockpot and set it on low, but my spidey senses continued to tingle as I reached for the keys. I put them back in the tray and went to the kitchen. "What, dad?" I said to the empty house. I looked at the crockpot to find flames licking up the side from the cord. "NOOOOOO!" I screamed, then pulled the cord from the outlet and smothered the flames with a dish towel.

Stunned, I took a moment to thank my dad for saving me from the tragedy of a house fire since I was about to leave for errands and not return for hours. After the adrenaline wore off, I started crying as hard as I did when dad died a decade before. The Rival had performed beautifully in its 40+ years of service, but letting it go was like letting go of dad all over again. Seeing the avocado green beauty sitting on the kitchen counter each time I made the meatballs and hearing the familiar rattle of the glass lid allowed me to feel closer to dad. The crockpot wasn't just an appliance; it was the ultimate symbol of love that mended my relationship with my dad.

I called Bill while he was driving and incoherently explained the tragedy. "Fire!" I cried, but couldn't get any more words out as I bawled. He was distraught, thinking the house had burned and that I was hurt. I calmed down enough to explain that I was safe and had prevented the spread of flames, but he immediately understood how devastated I was at the loss. "Food is love no matter where or how it's prepared," he told me.

Food is love, no matter where or how it's prepared.

I wiped off dad's crockpot and set it in the basement. When I remodeled my kitchen in 2018, I set the crockpot on an open shelf in honor of my dad. I now have two other Rival crockpots of different sizes that perform beautifully and cook the meatballs to perfection each time. Bill was right about it not mattering where or how a meal is prepared. Food is love.

23

Leslie Hart-Davidson

"I only make these for people I love," is what I say to folks when I feed them Jim Hart's meatballs. I'll be up front in telling you that ballification is a labor of love and will take a hot minute to get going. Once you spend the morning assembling the sauce and balls, you can nestle the balls in their liquid bliss in the crock pot and let them rock on their own until dinner-time. I pinky swear it'll be worth it.

Meatballs

2 lb fresh ground beef (85-90% lean)
3 slices toasted wheat or seedy bread, cut into itty bitty cubes
2 eggs
2 tsp horseradish
1 tsp garlic powder
¾ tsp salt
½ tsp allspice
¾ tsp nutmeg
1 tsp dried oregano
2 tsp ground pepper
2 TB worchestershire
1 TB ketchup
1 small onion, finely diced
⅓ C evoo for browning

Sauce

1 46 oz can/jar tomato juice
1 6 oz can Italian style tomato paste
1 15 oz can tomato puree
1 tsp garlic salt
2 tsp sweet basil
2 tsp sugar
1 tsp brown sugar

(continued on next page)

Serves: 6
Pairs with: nostalgia & people you love.
Note: don't burn your balls or they'll ruin the sauce.

The leftover balls make incredible sandwiches, especially when melted cheese is added

25

Bring the tomato juice to a boil in a large pan, then lower to a simmer until reduced by 1/3 (about 20 minutes). In a crock pot set on low, mix together the remaining sauce ingredients, then pour in the tomato juice.

While the tomato juice is reducing, whisk together the eggs with the spices and wet ingredients in a large bowl. Add the ground beef, then plop in the teeny tiny toasted bread cubes and diced onion.

If you're squicked out by touching raw meat, grab a plastic glove or a large plastic storage baggie and shove your hand inside like a haphazard food condom. Mix the crap out of the beef goo until you're confident that the mixture is blended (or until your hand hurts. Either one.)

Prepare a non-stick skillet with a tablespoon or two of evoo and turn heat to medium. To form the balls, grab a plate to stage the meatballs ready to be browned and another lined with paper towels to receive the completed ones. Using a tablespoon, grab a chunk of meat mixture about golf ball size with your dominant hand and place it in your other hand. Use the tablespoon to form the ball, rolling it around until uniform. Place on the staging plate until full.

To brown the balls, roll the evoo around the pan to cover the bottom. Imagine the pan as a clock and begin placing the balls at 6pm, moving clockwise and making a second ring inside if necessary (about 12 balls maximum). Jiggle the pan when all are placed to prevent sticking. Check the heat and browning level after one minute. Using tongs, start at 6pm again and flip each ball in the order you placed them and adjust heat if necessary.

Repeat the flip two more times, turning to a fresh side to brown each time. When the balls are uniformly browned, remove to the paper towel lined plate.

Continue the browning with the next batch, adding more oil or stopping to wipe out any burned bits if necessary. When all the balls are browned, lovingly spoon each ball into the crock pot tomato bath, softly pressing each down into the liquid to make room for the next. Cook for at least 4 hours on high or up to 10 hours on low, stirring frequently with a gentle hand.

Serve with spaghetti and Waldorf salad.

After stirring, try dipping wavy potato chips in the sauce. My mama and I would do that every time Jim Hart made meatballs, much to his dismay.

27

Leslie Hart-Davidson

why give is my religion

I am the child of an excommunicated Catholic father and a quasi-Christian mother. My big brother celebrated his first communion shortly after I was born. My mother, having schlepped him to classes and events in preparation for this event that was important to my father, declared that she was done with religion. I don't have the luxury of asking her if that decision was fueled by the inconvenience of classes or the overabundance of masses since she died a decade ago, but I do know that what guided her morality was a sense of kindness and generosity. "Don't be a jerk," she'd tell me when I was younger. Mom radiated kindness daily as she navigated the world, so it wasn't hard to shake the feeling that the very *least* I could do was not be a dick. Other friends had Disapproving Jesus as their spiritual guide who kept them in check. I had Mary Hart's heavy gaze to guide me.

Dad was a devout Catholic despite his two divorces that rendered him persona non grata with the church. A kind priest allowed him to continue going to mass and eventually presided over his funeral. Dad shared Mom's ideology of kindness and was quick to offer assistance to complete strangers. There wasn't a day in his life when he didn't go out of his way to make someone smile or help them out. I don't know if his faith led him to kindness, or if my mother's influence made him more aware of opportunities to be a genuinely good human being. Perhaps both. The result was the same: marinating in a big, juicy, consistent bowl of everyday acts of kindness from my parents helped me develop my own religion. I call this religion GIVE.

28

Here's how I define Give:

> **Give:** n. \'giv\
> 1. Mindset that allows a person to think of others before themselves
> 2. Practical method for walking through life with a level of awareness for others that ultimately brings peace and joy to your own life
> 3. Ultimate expression of love that is offered to others by any form or means with zero expectation of return
> 4. The opposite of Take

Joey Tribianni from Friends had an interesting theory on the philosophy of Give. In the episode "The one Where Phoebe Hates PBS," Joey had this line of questioning when Phoebe stated that doing good deeds for others was a selfless act:

"Well yeah, it was a really nice thing and all, but it made you feel really good, right? ...well it made *you* feel good, so that makes it selfish...There's no unselfish good deed. Sorry."

Joey has an important point about why we're motivated to Give. If there is truly no such thing as an unselfish good deed, then our motivation is to feel the happiness that results from the act. Know what? That's just fine. Any motivation to Give is good.

We often place the interest of the other and the interest of self at opposites. It doesn't negate the value of generosity if you gain as well; it's still a gratuitous act. Here's the deal: good will is a not a finite resource. Ghandi didn't get to be Ghandi by being good to one person.
He gave and gave, making everyone better. There is **Give is not a finite resource.**

no need to ration non-finite things such as good will, reputation, and cheer. Like a Las Vegas buffet, there will always be more.

I wear Give like a piece of jewelry—a mental string around my finger—to remind me to make the world better and protect it from too much Taking. There is no limit to our capacity as humans to Give, so check out these rules to get started:

1. **Just Give**
   When my daughter was born in 2005, it leveled up my capacity to love. I looked at the baby bean wrapped in a scratchy striped hospital blanket and knew I would do anything, ANYTHING for this tiny human. Lillian grew at the same astounding rate as my love for her. I would frequently joke that I would gladly find a sharp knife, cut open my chest and rip out my still-beating heart to hand her on a silver platter if that would make her happy. Even in her challenging teenage years, I still offer that up. I offer to protect her, care for her, encourage her, and sacrifice things that I need or want in order to ensure her health and happiness. That right there? That is Give.

   Give is the desire to help, encourage, uplift, maintain, spend time with, care for and bring joy to others with zero expectation of return. It's easiest to explain Give from a parental perspective. Why do we Give as parents? Part of the reason could be an evolutionary imperative in order to keep the youngins alive for the sake of the species. The other part could be from the oxytocin released in our brains when we nurture and care for them. Either way, the biological and moral reasons work together for a positive outcome that just feels good when we Give.

Give within the immediate family is how most folks first learn of the concept. It's easy to be kind and generous to the people you live with, but it's not always obvious that treating the rest of humanity that way could be a thing as well. Jim and Mary Hart did an amazing job of transferring their familial Give to the rest of the world, so it was second nature for me to extend the same criteria of care to others: friends, coworkers, random strangers and even animals all fit under the umbrella of Give. It felt normal and right to be good to others.

As my circle of family dwindles from death, my capacity to Give grows. The more loss I experience, the greater my desire to do good. It's the only method I know for managing grief and moving forward.

2. **When in doubt, Give more**
   "Love is not a finite emotion.
   We don't have only so much to share.
   Our hearts create love as we need it."
   — Dan Brown, Origin

Let me be clear in this whole business of Give: you will never run out of love. Your heart will never be empty. Every action of kindness in the name of Give will come back to you tenfold. The love you use when you Give is an endless supply that regenerates like crazy. Like bunnies. Like Tribbles. There is NO reason to hoard your love, so when you Give, ask yourself this: "Can I do more?"

The "more" part of that question refers to any resource other than love. When you get to a point in your Give journey when the love part seems intuitive and easy, start considering what additional resources you have

31

in order to Give. How about your time? Expertise? Advice? Kindness? Money? Whenever and wherever you can, at every opportunity, offer it up. Hold the door for folks when entering or leaving a building (Hodor would thank you). Take your cart back into the store after shopping. Smile at a baby. Be patient in line at the grocery. Let a car merge without sighing or judging. Donate blood. Volunteer at an organization that is meaningful to you. Send money to reputable causes. Walk the dogs at a local animal shelter. **Any** altruistic act is a form of Give. When you ask yourself if you've done enough and you have any doubt at all, Give more.

The most important thing to remember in all of these actions is that there is NO expectation of return when it comes to Give. Zero. Zip. Know why? Give with expectation of return is TAKE, and takers will be harshly judged by Mary Hart (or Disapproving Jesus, if that's your jam.)

3. **Fuck Take**

There are essentially three different varieties of Takers in the world that rally against the concept of Give, whether unintentionally, selfishly or maliciously. I refer to this Take Trinity as Eeyores, Debbie Downers, and Martyrs.

Eeyores are the most benign of the Take Trinity who wield the prepositions "to" and "at" like weapons. Their immediate instinct is to not only think the very worst of a situation or individual, but to share it on social media or with others in person to bring full attention to their plight.

"My date cancelled on me last minute, so I might as well give up on ever finding love."

"The stupid worker in the drive through gave me onion on my burger when I told him NO ONION. FML I can't ever get what I want!"
Eeyores are difficult to cheer up and often prefer venting over making any strides to remedy a situation. Their defeatist attitudes are a perfect storm for screaming into the void that is social media.

Debbie Downers suck the life out of the room by practicing Take when it comes to happiness. Rachel Dratch made the term famous during a recurring *Saturday Night Live* skit where she related to her friends' conversations with a negative spin or contrary story that dismissed the validity of their happiness. Debbie Downers are a more malicious version of Eeyores in that they actively rob people of joy for no reason.

> You are enjoying your day, everything is going your way, then along comes Debbie Downer.

"I don't want a piece of your birthday cake. Refined sugar is causing an epidemic of juvenile diabetes in this country."

"It's too bad that a tree fell on your car during the last storm. Puerto Rico still has thousands of homeless people after the hurricane."

Martyrs are sneakiest of the Take Trinity because their actions are wrapped in what they feel are good intentions. Sinister giving allows Martyrs to give, but with a catch. A price tag. Strings attached. Sometimes the Giving act requires monetary or in-kind payback:

"I'm going to give you a ride to the hospital to visit your friend, but you need to run in the store on the way there and get these five things for me."

Leslie Hart-Davidson

Sometimes the Giving act exacts an emotional toll:
"I woke up two hours early to make this amazing meal that takes all day to cook, and you decide to be late to dinner? Honestly, I don't even know why I bother taking care of this family if all you ever do is deny my love."

Martyrs often combine the first two types of Takers by insisting on venting and robbing others of a joyful moment that they themselves instigate through a veiled act of Give. "Yes, I'll do this for you (even if you didn't ask for it) BUT" is the standard operating procedure for this group of Karens on the Cross.

It's easy to read through the list of Takers and identify someone in your life who has exhibited one of those behaviors. Usually, spending time with Takers leaves you feeling a little less motivated, joyful and positive about the future of humanity. Some high-level takers can leave a psychic residue on you after being in their presence that makes you want to shower to get the ick off.

Here's an important question: do you have the oves to turn that gaze inward? Think about all of your behaviors and actions during the day that could be interpreted as one of the Take Trinity: did you cut in line? Poo poo an idea? Badmouth someone? Eat the last donut? Fail to refill the toilet paper? Did you assume that your needs were always greater than someone else's and that you deserve more credit or attention than they do? Don't be a Taker. Fuck Take.

4. **Remember that you are not more important that the next person**
The day my brother passed away from a lengthy illness at The James Cancer Research Center in Ohio, I sat quietly with him and made all of

Food is Love

the important phone calls to family members. After a few hours dealing with the bureaucracy and finality of death, I remember saying this during the call to my business manager/dear friend Jen: "Just tell me what to do. I don't know what to do now." She asked the last time I had eaten and I couldn't remember. Knowing my deep love of the Ohio classic Skyline chili, she texted me the location of the nearest restaurant. "Go there. Go eat. Now."

I wiped my tears and drove to Skyline. The manager greeted me and handed me a menu. "Sorry I'm not as cheery as I could be today," he apologized. "My washing machine broke this morning and that's about the last thing I needed. It's been the worst day—you just can't imagine!"

The moment I heard the manager's woes, I figured I had three different ways I could process it. First, I could ignore him and just order my food. Second, I could reply with the Queen Mum of all "OH YEAH?!" trump cards and vomit my morning's heartache all over his washing machine woes. My third option, however, was to Give by being supportive. I looked the manager in the eyes and told him that I hoped his day would get much better. I told him that I would think good things for him and his appliance repairs. And I told him that I was super hungry and would love to leave him a big tip if he brought me delicious food quickly.

The Skyline manager got a big tip that day, and I got a big opportunity to remind myself that I'm not more important than others.

5. **Practice "with and for," not "to and at"**
Prepositions play an important role in the English language by linking and showing connections in a clause. I like to think about living my life

through prepositions: carefully selected and curated words that show my intention of Give.

The prepositions "with" and "for" are the opposite of "to" and "at" in my Give language. For example, talking at people is an intention to spew your ideas towards them with no interest of reciprocity. A colloquial Ohio thing to say is "I'll talk ATcha later," which is a sweet way of ending a conversation that isn't viewed as equal. After a hometown friend called me and spent thirty minutes going on about her latest medical issues and in-law feuds without once asking me how I was, I listened patiently and gave her as much time as I had available that day. I told her that I had to scoot and pick up my daughter from school. "I'll have to talk atcha later," I offered.

Conversations can be significantly more engaging and helpful when the opposite preposition is engaged: with. Good-intentioned conversations are born from the idea of talking with others. "With" is a partnership during the exchange of words, whereas "at" is lobbing words catapult-style towards another.

The "to" and "for" prepositions show opposite intentions as well. Interpret the meaning of the sentence "I'm going to do something TO you" versus "I'm going to do something FOR you." Doing something TO you could be pretty maniacal; I could intend to give you a swirlie in the toilet or cut a bitch. Doing something FOR you has the opposite connotation; you might get excited to think about what's about to happen. Are you going to bake me a cake? Buy me a bike? Do my laundry? Oh, the happy possibilities are endless! Staying in the mindset of doing tasks FOR others is a happier place to be in a world of Give.

6. **Just do the next right thing**
The philosophy of Give can be overwhelming if it's not how your brain works. Sometimes it's best not to overthink it or turn it into a lifestyle or mantra. Think about it this way: if you're unhealthy due to excess pounds, it may seem incredibly challenging to suddenly start a diligent exercise routine and completely upend your eating routine. Success may not always come to those who have so very much to change all at once. Dipping a toe in the health-conscious water is a good way to start, though: walking a bit each day and swapping sodas for water can lead to a better outcome long-term.

The next right thing is helpful to think about in the same small step scenario. If you can't wrap your brain around the whole philosophy of Give, you can just think about the next action or reaction that feels kind as you navigate the world. There's no need to think about your legacy of kindness from a 10,000 foot view; just look at what's in your face at the moment and do something nice for someone. Empathy is a THING.

7. **At the very least, don't be a dick**
My teenage daughter is fluent in the language and nuances of Give. I won't kid you; Lillian is a typical teen and can be a righteous asshat some days. However, she benefitted from the Jim and Mary Hart school of Give and has witnessed the power of being a good human to all in her path since the day she was born. I took a page from a coworker of mine knowing that it could alleviate some of the pressure of growing up in a Give-intensive home.

Decades ago, that coworker had teenage children who were overachievers stressfully navigating high school in an affluent area. This was the era before helicopter parenting and social media, so she and her husband utilized a rather unorthodox three-rule system for their kids:

1. No drunk driving
2. No diseases
3. No grandchildren

My coworker explained that ruling by consequence rather than distinction allowed the kids to make free-range behavior choices. "I didn't tell them they couldn't drink," she explained. "Nor did I tell them they couldn't fool around. I just made them understand that their decisions would impact the rest of their lives and help shape them as people." Her kids turned out great.

When my husband and I dropped off Lillian at music camp in the summer of 2019, we gave her the laundry list of things that she could accomplish outside of the choir room during her intensive ten days as a third-time alum: being a good mentor to the younger campers, being a good friend to the homesick kids, and being an aid to the professors. "Ohmygawwwwwwd you guysuuuuuhhhh," she replied. "You're pressuring me SO MUCH!" I channeled my coworker's theory of consequence combined with Wil Wheaton's law and offered up a different approach. "Bean," I said. "Just don't be a dick."
"Deal," she said.

Lillian accomplished everything and more that we asked of her during that music session. As the grandchild of Jim and Mary Hart, I think she's making them proud through Give.

Give

a handy guide for being a good human

Leslie Hart-Davidson

Food insecurity is shitty. My mom did her level best to keep my belly full after school as inexpensively as possible. One afternoon I asked her to make me spaghetti with pasta sauce like I had enjoyed at a friend's house. We didn't have any jar sauce, so ketchup sketti was born. Mom used watered down ketchup and sprinkled in dried basil to fancy it up a bit as she warmed the makeshift sauce on the stove. "It's the best I can do, LC." she said as she handed me the bowl. "It's perfect," I replied.

Despite all the culinary badassery in my arsenal, I still make this when I'm missing my mama just to feel closer to her. Food is love, after all.

ketchup sketti
the government thinks ketchup is a vegetable

1 bunch of spaghetti noodles about dime size in diameter
¼ C ketchup
3 TB water
1 TB dried basil

Cook pasta according to package directions and drain. In a microwave safe bowl, combine the ketchup, water and basil with a good stir. Nuke it for about 45 seconds and remove.

Plop the cooked pasta into the bowl and toss to coat evenly.

Serves: 1
Pairs with: conversations about class migration.
Complexity: Patrick Star could do it.

the how & why of cooking

I snorted my green tea as I read this Ina Garten meme about butter. I'm a HUGE fan of both Ina and the Food Network. I love watching her create beautiful, tasty meals with zero concern for timing in her immaculate kitchen with a seemingly endless supply of prep bowls. While I would love to have a kitchen stadium as shiny and well-stocked as Ina's, I'm perfectly content in my farm kitchen with enough counter space for my cutting board and bottle of wine. The space is cozy thanks to an island made from a salvaged university library desk where family and friends gather so I can feed them.

My twenty-something cousin visited one summer and re-marked that we had entertained more guests in her 8 week stay than her parents had entertained in her lifetime.

Since the island is "right up in my bidness" in the kitchen, I'm only one step away from my feedlings as I'm preparing meals. My kitchen is a stage, and I'm cool with that. I know that many of you read that last line and are cringing at the thought of having people watch you as you make a holy mess while cooking and have the added pressure of entertaining while trying to multitask a meal. I get it—not everybody wants an audience while they're cooking, and not everybody wants to cook for their family regularly. That's perfectly fine. After years of living the "food is love" philosophy and seeing firsthand how much happiness it can create, I wanted to write this book to encourage folks to look at cooking differently. Not a chore, not a hobby, but just...love.

Every concept I talk about in this book and all the recipes I'll offer are doable, attainable, and practical (plus full of snark and naughty words, because *salty lass*). I'm not a professional cook, but I am a professional interior designer and will use my knowledge to help you understand how your kitchen space directly impacts your ability to store, prepare, cook and clean up after meals.

"We eat with our eyes" is a common phrase that describes the importance of presentation and plating. I reinterpreted two primary concepts from *Remodeling Your House without Killing Your Spouse* and *It's Not Your Room, it's You* called CRAP and TALC to better explain the role of function and aesthetics when it comes to cooking and serving food. These acronyms are handy reminders to help you diagnose and treat the kitchen or other spaces in your home that feel just a little off.

I want to offer a bit of clarity here: if you're new to the LHD scene and haven't read my other books, you should know a few things about me. First, I'm a real person, not a persona. I'd gladly sit and have a beer with you to explain why I love food and design (and perhaps why I love bacon so much that I put a blond highlight in my red hair to make it look like porktastic goodness). However, I am painfully aware that when I post food porn incessantly on social media that the reaction is anywhere from "omg that looks amazing!" to "you bitch, why are you taunting me?!" to "I can never have food that good." Here's the thing: I possess the five key ingredients (pun totally intended) to make daily cooking for my family and design staff a possibility: desire, time, resources, motive and know-how.

Leslie Hart-Davidson

My **desire** to cook is deep and real. I'm fortunate to have an insanely grateful husband with zero picky tendencies. I also have a staff of hungry college interns at HDD Studios who will literally eat anything I put in front of them (bonus that it's not Ramen!) so my audience is an appreciative one. My amazing business manager JJ negotiated food as part of her compensation package, so I cook on a bigger scale and with great intention.

Time is a critical factor in cooking regularly. Get ready to want to punch me in the face: I live 17 steps from work. My design studio is a ten second commute, so I can run back to the main house and stir shit in the crock pot or snap beans or thaw something during the day. The proximity is useful on days that I'm local, but my schedule can be wonky otherwise with site visits to clients and days that I have tv appearances on the other side of the state. I make it work on the busiest days with proper planning so that I don't fall into the "let's just get take-out" trap.

Okay, you can definitely face punch me for this one: I am fortunate to have ridiculous **resources** for selecting and cooking meals. There are three stellar grocery stores and three high-quality butcher shops within 4 miles of my home. I know most of the cashiers by name and have solid relationships with the dudes who supply my junky-level carnivorous tendencies. Beyond the groceries, I've also cultivated an amazing stock of cookware, tools and knives over the last 20+ years and get to use them in a functional kitchen whose space I enjoy. I fully understand that not everyone has these resources, but I'll cheerfully admit that it does make my cooking life easier. Does that mean that you're off the hook if you don't have awesome grocery stores and cookware and a fabulous kitchen? Nope. Any cooking is an act of love.

Food is Love

My **motive** for cooking is pretty straightforward: I don't want to die. Let me try to rephrase that—most of my family has passed. I consider it an obligation to my husband, daughter, remaining family and friends to be healthy and do everything in my power to stay on the earth a little longer. Eating out too much or making shitty convenience-only decisions about food just wrecks me. I'll explain more shortly about how I completely changed how I cook for my family after a health scare with my husband, but please know that I view food as a long-term investment in health.

Finally, my **know-how** of cooking techniques and processes allows me to whip up a single dish or an oh-shit level of impromptu dinner party for 12 people (yes, I've totally rocked that). How did I gain that knowledge? I learned early what things were possible in the kitchen from my parents, my amazing mother-in-law, incredibly talented friends, the Food Network, and craptons of trial and error. Each new dish was an opportunity to practice techniques and allow for more exploration and creativity.

I promise you that anybody can learn to cook, and you can actually love to cook when you have the combination of desire, time, motive, resources and know-how at any level.

45

My business manager Jen went on vacation when she was young and stayed at a small family-owned motel. The lobby was empty when her folks tried to check in, but she heard the dad talking to his daughter in the room behind the desk. The daughter asked a series of questions that so annoyed the dad that he finally shouted "I DON'T KNOW, CASSIE. I REALLY DON'T FUCKING KNOW!" Jen gasped, causing the hotel owner to turn around red-faced.

Thanks to that fun exchange, the correct answer to anything we're unsure of in the studio is "Cassie." "What's for lunch, Les?" Jen will ask. "Cassie-role," I tell her.

hash brown casserole
a pan full of cheesey carbs is what my uterus needs right now.

1 20 oz package fresh shredded hash browns
1 8 oz package diced ham
1 C sour cream
¾ C milk
2 C white cheese
(mozzarella or italiany blend)
2 C colby jack cheese
1 TB ranch dip powder

Directions

Preheat the oven to 375 degrees. In a large bowl, plop in the sour cream, milk and seasonings and whisk until combined. Add the diced ham and stir until the pork clumps are distributed evenly.

Add two cups of your favorite white cheese (mozzarella, Italian blend, etc) and stir. Finally, add the potatoes and fold it together.

Turn the mixture into a 9 x 13 Pyrex pan and top with remaining cheese. Cover with foil and bake for 50 minutes. Remove the foil and crank the heat in the oven to gently brown the top layer of cheese. Broil for 2-3 minutes if you'd like the top layer a bit crunchy.

Allow to cool for 10-15 minutes if you can stand it. Serve in cute little 4" squares, or just grab a giant serving spoon and stick your face near the pan and go to town. No judgement here.

46

Serves: 6-8
Pairs with: PMS and chocolate chaser.
Consideration: you'll definitely overeat this.

Thanks to its simplicity in ingredients and ease of preparation, this crock pot meal is a favorite of my HDD Studios interns. It's ready for lunch if started first thing in the morning, and the leftovers are hella-delicious. Serve with yellow rice and some veggies for a complete meal, or try them as sliders for an awesome leftover snack.

honey mustard chicken

what's in it? honey + mustard + chicken.

8 boneless, skinless chicken thighs
⅓ C stone ground mustard
⅓ C evoo
⅓ C honey
¼ C (half stick) melted butter

Serves: 6
Pairs with: a brillo pad for your crock pot.
Complexity: Homer Simpson could make this.

Grab the crock pot and turn to the low setting. Plop in the mustard, evoo and honey in that order (so the honey doesn't stick to the measuring cup). Melt the butter and pour that in too, then whisk until combined.

Nestle the chicken thighs in the sauce, turning to coat. If you're nearby and can check them after a few hours, give them a good stir. After about 4 hours on low, take a potato masher or large fork and mush the fall-aparty chicken until the sauce is evenly distributed among the chunks.

using chicken breasts in-
stead of thighs reduces
cooking time by an hour

49

wo things are true of this delightful porktastic dish: in order to properly enjoy it, you need to be both carnivorous annnnnd hungry AF. Don't take on creating this meal unless you're in the mood to eat heavy and enjoy a ton of intense flavor. The best it has ever tasted for me was after a day of burning 1,000 calories from shoveling my giant circular driveway during a big snowstorm.

2.5 lbs country style boneless pork ribs
1 18 oz bottle Sweet Baby Ray's bbq sauce
5 large sweet potatoes
2 cups Brussels sprouts
1 can chicken stock
2 TB butter
4 TB evoo
Salt & pepper

Serves: a small army.
Pairs with: stupid cold days in the winter. Also, Mashed Sweet Potatoes and Browned Spouts on the next page.

Sweet talk your butcher into cutting you bigass, beautiful boneless pork ribs. Thank him or her kindly, then take them home and unceremoniously dump them in a giant crock pot (wider crocks work better than the taller ones for this). Open the bottle of bbq sauce (you can use whichevs brand you like, but not one with high sugar content as it will burn) and pour it all over the ribs. Mush the ribs and sauce around until coated, then Ron Popeil that bitch (set it on low and forget it).

(continued on next page)

rib-tacular stack
I'm full-time fancy now.

Okay, I lied. You can't forget it. Mix and mush a few hours in to break up the ribs in little pieces. Potato mashers work great for that, but a giant fork works well too. 6 hours-ish on low is good overall.

Mashed Sweet Potatoes: peel the taties and cube them. Dump in a pan with a can of chicken stock and enough water to just cover the tasty spuds. Cook on high until the liquid evaporates, then take off the heat and add the butter pats. Salt to taste, then mix the shit out of them with a spoon.

Sprouts: cut the butts off the sprouts and slice them in half. Steam in the microwave for a couple minutes to soften, then drain well and toss in a pan over medium high heat with 4TB evoo and salt & pepper. Push them around for a few until some of the bits start to caramelize.

Stack the deliciousness in this order (because cute): a base of sweet potato mash that's flatted out, a scoop of sprouts that nestle in the spuds, and a plop of ribs with some BBQ goo. If you're one of those people who can't have their food touching, my six year old self silently weeps with you (and wants you to GET OVER IT).

Note: if you'd like to double down on the pork in this meal, feel free to cook two slices of bacon in a pan until crisp. Remove the bacon and all but a few TB of the grease. Crumble the pieces and set aside. Add the sprouts to the bacon grease and cook until caramelized, then add the bacon crumbles back in and stir.

prosciutto-bound asparagus
your pee is gonna smell soooooo funny.

M y pal Mike introduced me to the joy of wrapping things with porktastic goodness years ago. Melon, corn on the cob, and various veggies just minding their own business being healthy and stuff were suddenly transformed into glorious bites of salty, fatty heaven.

Asparagus is a perfect recipient of the prosciutto treatment because of its similar cooking time. 30ish minutes in the oven at high heat yields a crisp porky wrap around perfectly al dente asparagus spears. Serve on a bed of yellow rice for a lovely meal.

1 bunch fresh asparagus spears
(about #2 pencil diameter)
1 package prosciutto
(about 5 oz)
3 T evoo
Salt and pepper to taste

Directions

Preheat the oven to 425 degrees. Rinse the asparagus carefully and cut the woody bottoms off to a uniform length. Take each slice of prosciutto and carefully tear it apart lengthwise to make 2 strips. Starting at the tip, wrap the prosciutto strip snugly around the asparagus stalk. Continue until the strips run out.

Place the wrapped stalks in a Pyrex baking dish and surround them with any remaining naked stalks. Drizzle the evoo over the asparagus and shimmy the dish to ensure the oil is evenly distributed so that the stalks won't stick to the pan.

Bake for 30ish minutes until the asparagus spears are fork-tender. Serve over a bed of rice.

Serves: 4
Pairs with: a sharp knife and a big glass of water.
Consideration: easy bougie meal to impress guests.

A drizzle of balsamic
glaze tastes amazeballs

55

The happiest carbs of all in my world are these ridonkulously flavorful, completely addictive mashed potatoes. I'll ruin you for all other spuds once you've experienced the depth of **there** there with this recipe.

The secret is a combo of the perfectly textured Yukon gold potatoes and the swapping of standard tap water with chicken stock for boiling the spuds. Here's the coolest thing that I learned thanks to Jim Hart: don't drain the potatoes. The stock slowly evaporates while infusing the spuds with a flavor that will knock your socks off.

crack mashed taties
oh yeah. i'd mainline these bad boys.

3 lbs Yukon gold potatoes, peeled and diced
1 14 oz can chicken stock (about 1 ½ C)
¼ C butter, sliced into pats for easy melting
½ C milk or cream (if desired)
2 tsp salt

Serves: 6
Pairs with: Two hours on the elliptical machine.
Consideration: soak your pan STAT to curb crusting.

Peel the potatoes and cut into 1" or smaller chunks. Rinse in a colander, then place in a large pot with a can of chicken stock and enough water to juuust cover the top of the chunks. Turn the heat to medium high and boil for 20ish minutes, reducing the heat to medium low as the chicken stock begins to evaporate. When the potatoes begin to hiss as all the liquid disappears, turn the heat to low and smush with a potato masher, adding the butter pats and salt. Taste as you go, adding milk or cream in small bits to get the consistency and flavor you like.

Note: If you'd like to channel your own 50 year old Sally O'Malley and KICK and PUNCH these crack taties to a new level, add a teaspoon of horseradish. They're incredible served with meatloaf.

Richard Dreyfus
challenges you
to build with
your taties

57

spectrum of fucks

Fucks = a unit of care currency that can be spent as the fuck-holder deems worthy or not spent at all. Fucks are more precious than gold, more stable than the U.S. dollar, and more real than Bitcoin.

All of us have access to a certain number of fucks at various points in our lives. What's a fuck? I define fucks as a unit of care that can be spent as the holder of the fuck deems worthy. Unlike love (which is infinite), the unit of care in a fuck is a finite resource that only regenerates with time, rest and mental clarity.

Much like the Seinfeld character Elaine Benes found only certain male partners to be "sponge-worthy" based on the preciousness of the contraceptive resource, the holder of fucks can choose whether to spend or save their unit of care in any way and for any reason. While giving zero fucks can be an act of self-preservation, giving a fuck can be generous and loving: a true act of Give.

Since our fucks are a resource, it's best to think about them as currency. Let's call them fuck bucks. We have a certain amount of fuck bucks that we can spend in a situation, so budgeting appropriately

Food is Love

is important. The trick is to reserve our fucks for the meaningful things in life instead of the trivial ones that try to suck up our attention.

Please know this about fucks related to food: I give zero judgy fucks about how you get a meal on the table for your family. Budgeting your fucks appropriately allows you to embrace the idea of Food is Love by NOT spending your fucks on excuses for avoiding cooking. Here are some ideas to budget your cooking fucks wisely:

1. **Be present in your presentation**
    When you give zero fucks about being pressured from Pinterest or Food Network or the Tasty recipes on Facebook to make beautiful, complicated, social-post-worthy meals, you can instead concentrate on the WHO and the WHY to create a worthy meal experience.

2. **Meet the food where it's at**
    It's okay if you live in a food desert or the ingredient you want is out of season or you honestly can't afford the grocery list required by the recipe. Doing the best you can with what is budgeted and available is still an act of love through cooking.

3. **Improvise! Adapt! Overcome!**
    Your prep/cooking spaces shouldn't hold you back from creating meals for your loved ones. You're willing to cook over a fire while camping, right? If you can figure out how to make food with fire, you can figure out how to carve out some prep space to make a decent meal.

Leslie Hart-Davidson

C heese is hands down my first pick as a desert island food. Throw in the cute factor of the adorable tiny size and my heart goes pitter-pat.

Part of the reason I love baby cheese coins so much is their versatility and ability to make people happy. These melted dairy delights can be used as a garnish for soups, a replacement for croutons, or a party tray item. I've watched with glee as my guests' faces light up when I offer them the bite-sized coins, so try serving them at your next gathering to be the hero your party needs.

2 C shredded parmesan cheese
(packaged or grated from a block)
1 ½ tsp garlic powder
1 tsp dried oregano
1 tsp dried basil
½ tsp ground pepper

Preheat the oven to 425 degrees. In a bowl, mix the parmesan shreds and spices with a fork. On a parchment lined baking sheet, spoon out quarter-sized scoops of the mixture about 1" apart. Bake for 8-10ish minutes until golden brown, rotating the pan halfway through. Allow to cool on the baking pan before serving.

Makes: 15-20 coins
Pairs with: LOTS and lots of willpower.
Consideration: these are adorable garnishes for soups.

don't use the
powdered shit
in a shaky can

61

ince I began the college student internship program in 2006 for my design company, HDD Studios, I've been feeding my students. When the kids would express an interest in cooking, I'd arrange lessons and teach them. Recently, my awesome intern Becca flipped the script and taught *me* one of her family recipes.

For Becca, sloppy joes were the first meal that she learned to cook with her dad in fourth grade. The busy school year filled with activities pulling her whole family in different directions put this easy sloppy joe recipe with minimal clean-up in heavy rotation.

becca's sloppy joes
cue Chris Farley and Adam Sandler.

2 lbs 90% ground beef
6 oz Sweet Baby Ray's regular bbq sauce (1/3 of small bottle)
3 TB ketchup
2 TB yellow mustard
1 tsp Sriracha sauce
1 tsp brown sugar
1 ½ tsp garlic powder
1 ½ tsp onion powder
1 ½ tsp Lawry's season salt

Makes: 6ish
Pairs with: The dread of a cold-ass soccer game.
Complexity: your kid can totally make this.

In a large nonstick skillet, brown the ground beef until no longer pink. Drain all but a smidge of the grease and return to a baby simmer. In a bowl, mix the bbq sauce, ketchup, mustard and sriracha. Toss in the brown sugar and remaining spices and stir well. Add the goo to the ground beef and stir around until combined and heated through.

Serving options include the carbilicious route of traditional bun, or plopping a pile of meaty goodness in a bowl using corn/tortilla chips or wavy potato chips as a scoop. Banana peppers rings are also a delightful garnish.

While not
photogenic, it's
delicious AF

Bucket List

Greg would spend the next week in the ICU building his strength enough to be released. Scores of specialists and aides came by to help prepare him for the big life adjustment of cancer treatment and tube feeding. His tumor, so obnoxiously and dangerously wrapped around his thyroid and trachea, was inoperable. As I watched each specialist come and go and Greg's head spin as a result of the medications and volume of information, I realized pretty quickly that I would need to be his advocate.

A few weeks after he was released from the hospital, I took Greg for the first oncologist visit to determine a care plan. The local oncologist was kind, but inexperienced. He carefully explained that the tumor was so involved that he didn't feel comfortable treating it. "You're stage four. We can't cure you, but if you have any shot at prolonging your life, it'll be with the folks at The James. Go there." In the parking lot of the oncology center after the appointment, Greg was quiet. "Drive to Schuler's," he said. "I'm not ready to go home yet." At the bakery, Greg bought me their famous gingerbread men and a bunch of cookies for my daughter. He couldn't swallow, but he could chew and spit out food just to get the taste. When we got back home, he decapitated a gingy while I asked him an important question. "Look," I began. "It's not the best news about your cancer. But right now, right this very minute, you're strong. You can go anywhere and do pretty much anything. So I want you to think hard about this: what's on your bucket list?"

Greg had always been a man of simple means. He lived a Spartan life and wanted for very little. When he did want something, he patiently saved up and bought it for himself. The last time he traveled was in 1994 to visit our cousin Tom in Key West. Giving him gifts, as you can imagine, was a challenge. What I had done for years was give him a supply of ketchup bottles (damn that boy loved ketchup on everything) and Jim Hart's meatballs. My husband would make him gingerbread cookies as well in the shape of Star Wars characters.

Needful things were not in my brother's general vocabulary, so when I asked him about his bucket list, his eyes grew wide. I expected him to reply with a request for another trip to Key West or possibly to visit Universal Studios in Orlando. "I think what I'd really like is a new pair of eyeglasses," he said. "Mine are twenty years old and an arm is missing." I hesitated, not sure if he was for real. "Seriously?" I said. "You can….aim…higher, ya know." I encouraged. "Okay, here's an idea," he said. "The new Terminator movie is being filmed soon. I'd love to visit the set." "There you go! That's better!" I cheered him on. "Let me see what I can do for you!" I was disappointed to learn that the filming would take place in Europe two months later. He had neither the passport nor the ability to wait that long. I asked if he wanted to make any other bucket list plans, but all he asked for was a copy of the latest Entertainment Weekly magazine the next time I picked up his medication and supplies. Greg simply did not want for things.

"Mom! Where are the pliers?" I yelled as I sat in front of the massive piece of furniture that was the RCA color television and watched Saturday morning cartoons. It's spring of 1979 and I'm trying to flip between stations to catch the commercial for the birthday gift I'm secretly coveting. "Check under the newspaper near the couch," Mom replied. I scooted my bum over the gold and orange shag carpeting and flung the paper out of the way, revealing the needle nosed pliers that were used to grab the nub and change the channel. My big brother Greg broke off the knob, so we're stuck with the plier method for now.

As I flipped from Bugs Bunny to Popeye, I'm rewarded with the image of my precious: a brightly colored Marx plastic Big Wheel. It was a beautiful piece of transportation that would be the envy of the Northridge cul-de-sac. I cringe, however, when I see that only boys ride the Big Wheel during the commercial. The girls take a secondary role, cheering on the riders from afar during a fierce competition or being the side chick that starts the race by throwing down her pretty scarf. "I'm more than a stupid scarf," I mumbled as I watched the Big Wheel zig and zag across the screen.

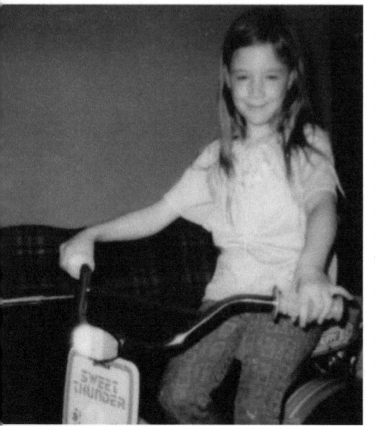

Armed with birthday cash from the grandparents a few weeks later, Mom took me to Kmart to shop. "Do you want another Barbie?" she asked. "I had something different in mind, actually," I told her. I led her out of the toy section toward the main aisle and stopped in front of the massive display of boxed Big Wheels, staring in wonder. "A Big Wheel?" she asked with alarm. "But you have a pink Sweet Thunder Huffy at home!" "I know," I began. "But this looks like so much fun!" "You can't put streamers on the Big Wheel, you know," Mom warned. "It's not about the streamers, Mom," I said. "It's about the Big Wheel."

Twenty minutes later, we loaded the Big Wheel in the trunk of her yellow Pontiac convertible and headed back to the cul-de-sac. When assembled later that day, I took off, flying around the neighborhood. The feel of the wind in my newly bobbed hairdo was just amazing. This was different from the Huffy; the world had a fascinatingly tactile perspective down low where you felt every sidewalk segment, every piece of gravel in the street, every twig you rolled over with the molded plastic wheels. It felt like empowerment. I liked this. I wanted more.

Shortly after I found the joy of the Big Wheel, I visited my friend Beth Ann a few blocks over from my house. When we were playing in her basement, I heard her older brothers conspiring about a neighborhood event and then take off quickly on their bikes. I stayed long enough to finish our game of Connect Four, then headed home. I rounded the corner of my street and heard shouts coming from the end of the cul-de-sac. I saw the source of the ruckus as I got closer to home: an epic Crash-up Derby between the Big Wheels and the Green Machines on the block. My stomach dropped as I saw my big brother Greg on my precious molded plastic piece of empowerment. He battled fiercely, crashing into the jerky neighbors and inflicting as much damage as possible. I was simultaneously proud of his skills and horrified that he abused my coveted Big Wheel.

When it was all over and victory was claimed by the Big Wheel crew, Greg returned to the garage with my precious vehicle. I inspected it carefully, noting all the scuffs and battle scars. "That's not so bad," I thought, then discovered the massive hole in the back molded tire. I let out a scream, then flopped down in the seat and fumed. I realized I'm sitting too far back since Greg adjusted the backrest to rumble. I flopped my limbs dramatically and let my head drop back. My pink Sweet Thunder Huffy loomed behind me, all of its girlish, streamered, non-battle-scarred charm beckoning me for an easy ride.

I sighed, adjusted the seat, and took off for a ride on my post-derby Big Wheel. It felt familiar, but a little off. Each tire rotation was noted by a rhythmic ka-THUD ka-THUD ka-THUD noise thanks to the tire hole. It still held the magic, though. It was still my Big Wheel.

Today at the Ohio State University when I took Greg to the oncologist, he needed a wheelchair to get him safely to the lab and the office on the 10th floor. As I wheeled him to the lab and had to navigate the furniture, I deviously leaned down and whispered "You know, I could fuck you up right now as payback for what you did to my Big Wheel when I was 7. You game for some Crash-up Derby?" The ear-to-ear grin on his face was my answer. I carefully delivered him to the appointment. Greg's body goes ka-THUD right now, but he still holds the magic. He's still my big brother.

why food matters

"A party without cake is just a meeting"
-Julia Child

Think for me about the most important events in life: birthdays, graduations, holidays, weddings, showers, funerals, family reunions. Want to know what they all have in common? People coming together to share experiences and...you guessed it...eat food. We bond over cake and fight over drumsticks and beg the cook for recipes. Food matters because it's the common denominator in all of life's events. You might loathe the politics of your creepy uncle, but you can both definitely agree that aunt Flo's vegan turkey gravy is about the worst shit you've ever had to fake-eat in your whole life.

While thinking about food and what an important role it has played for me (ya know, other than keeping me alive), I determined that food matters in six specific ways that I'd like to explain in more detail: medicine, connection, bonding, gifting, security and tradition. Let's explore each of these areas and their coordinating recipes.

Mama's 7th Birthday Party

Depression-era
Derr family picnic

Leslie Hart-Davidson

Grad school is a bitch. My husband Bill, who ran cross country in high school and was always fit, fell victim to the sedentary life of a graduate student when he entered his masters and then doctorate programs. Compounding that problem was my career in retail management during his grad school years that was dotted with wacky schedules, late night dinners and the need for complete convenience when it came to eating. I vividly remember calling home after closing up shop at 10pm and asking Bill what he'd like as I hit the Taco Bell drive thru week after week, year after year.

While we did enjoy cooking together when we had the time and opportunity, food at that point in our twenties was just shit-that-we-shoved-in-our-mouths. There was little planning or concern for health, because *twenties*. My career required that I walk many miles per day in the retail store, so I saw no direct effects from the shitty diet. Bill, however, began to very slowly gain weight.

Fast forward to our thirties. Bill was in a high-pressure new career as a professor, we relocated across the country, our families were dying off, we had a new baby, and he was at least 50 pounds heavier than his cross country days. At a yearly physical, Bill's doctor told him that he had type ll diabetes and high blood pressure that required medication. She explained something else important, though: that she knew he was smart, hard-working, and he had a choice. "I can prescribe metformin and lisinopril that you can take for the rest of your life and continue with your current lifestyle, dying as early as your relatives in the same boat. Or," she continued, "You can get off your ass, lose some weight, eat better, and never have to take drugs again. Your choice."

72

Realizing that his health was a long-term investment, Bill chose the second option. The doctor sent him to diabetes class where he met with a nutritionist for four hours to learn about appropriate serving sizes, carbohydrate units and calories. He listened carefully and brought home all the knowledge to rethink food.

Food became medicine for him. Our family cooking became more intentional, planned and balanced. We reinterpreted old dishes with healthier spins, fewer carbohydrates and realistic portion sizes. Better eating combined with Bill's new biking exercise regimen allowed him chuck the drugs after just a few months. He lost 50lbs in 7 months, and a total of 70lbs that year. It wasn't a diet; it was a way of life. More than a decade later, Bill has maintained the weight loss, run a marathon, participated in yearly Tour de Cure races, and completed multiple 100+mile bike rides. Most importantly, our cooking has remained the critical change that made us both ridiculously healthy.

I want to talk about an important detail for a hot minute. When Bill was originally diagnosed, we were living in a tiny rental home with a crappy little kitchen and a tight household budget thanks to our new tiny drooly human. To make significant changes in the way you cook and eat, it doesn't take granite countertops, a Wolf 6 burner range and a massive food budget; it only takes some nutritional education, a few feet of counter space and a decent knife and pan. Was it hard to give up Taco Bell and the gooey, salt-laden prepackaged meals we had eaten for a decade? Sure, at first. But after eating fresh, unprocessed food for a few months, my body summarily rejected convenience fare. Like Lindsey Buckingham, I'm never going back again.

Leslie Hart-Davidson

Growing up in the Midwest, "stew" always meant red meat with potatoes in a tomato base. When I first saw a version of this delicious dish, my thoughts ranged from "Squash isn't just for table decoration?" to "PEANUT BUTTER? WTAF?" I kicked up the spices a notch to make the dish even more Asian inspired with the garam masala, and I hope it's as shockingly tasty and delightful for you.

thai chicken & squash stew

WTF is a peanut butter slurry?!

3 TB EVOO
1 ½ lbs chicken tenders
1 medium onion, chopped
2 red bell peppers, diced
2 tsp minced garlic
2 cans chicken stock (14.5 oz cans, about 3 ½ C), divided
1 14 oz can diced tomatoes with juice
3 C 1" diced butternut squash (about 1 lb)
1 lb fresh green beans
Salt and pepper to taste
3 TB chili powder
3 TB garam masala
1 TB corn starch
¼ C creamy peanut butter
Cashews or peanuts for topping
Naan for slopping up the delightful sauce

Heat oil in a bigass pot. Add chicken, salt and pepper and sautée until the tenders are browned but not completely done. Remove to a plate. Reduce heat, then add onion, more salt, red bell pepper and garlic. Sautee for about 4 minutes until they're golden and pretty.

Add 3 ¼ C chicken stock (reserving ¼ cup for later) along with the can of tomatoes. Crank the heat and bring to a boil. While that's coming up to heat, cut the tenders across the grain so they kinda sorta shred. When the pot of deliciousness boils, add the chicken bits, squash and green beans. Your pot will look like it's overflowing, but I promise it will

74

Food is Love

don't dig cashews?
Swap for peanuts
or pumpkin seeds

Serves: 6
Pairs with: skeptics who want
their minds blown.
Consideration: this dish is a
gateway to all Thai food.

cook down. Just keep stirring to get all the bits coated in chicken stock and reduce the heat to medium, then pop on the lid and let it bubble for about 10 minutes. Stir occasionally (gently, please) as it boils down by about ¼ and the squash is tender.

While the pot is bubbling away, grab a bowl and prepare to give your arm a workout. Throw in the peanut butter, corn starch, and a bit of the ¼ C chicken stock. Whisky whisk and add more stock until the consistency is similar to heavy whipping cream. You want to be able to pick up the mixture with the whisk without it dribbling off like milk or sticking like frosting.

Reduce the heat to low and gently stir in the peanut butter mixture, chili powder and garam masala. After about 2 minutes, give it a taste and correct spices as needed. Serve with cashews or peanuts and naan to mop up the delightful sauce.

Bill's Food Medicine

Here's the big secret to treating food as medicine: simply pay attention to what you put in your pie hole. Being deliberate about what you eat will make you rethink mindlessly inhaling calories throughout the day. Success with eating healthier is all about being conscious of your food choices. Respect each bite you take as a worthwhile investment and you'll be well on your way to healthier eating.

In college when I lived off campus with several roommates, we always looked for easy and cheap meals to make. When Kroger had a sale on a ham chunk, I'd grab it and throw that in a crock pot with green beans and potatoes. After a long day of classes, it was great to come home to non-cafeteria, non-drive-thru food.

2 lbs cooked, sliced ham, cut into bite-sized chunks
3 lbs small red potatoes, cleaned and quartered
6 cups fresh green beans, snapped and halved
3 medium shallots, slivered
2 C chicken stock
1 tsp salt
2 tsp pepper

Toss the ingredients in a large crock pot, then give it a good stir. Cook for 4ish hours on high or 6ish hours on low.

Serves: 6
Pairs with: cold nights & Netflix benders.
Complexity: Homer Simpson could make this.

Zero judgement for using canned green beans and potatoes

In the early 80's, my folks went through a rough patch financially. The economy went to shit in my hometown, so dad packed us up and moved the family to North Carolina where he had heard better jobs were available. Spoiler alert: there weren't any better jobs available. We came back home after a few months, having depleted all savings and living in the last house my folks had tried to flip but were unable to sell.

Those few years were roughsauce. Luckily, my grandmother would drop by when needed, stocking the refrigerator with a few key items. We'd frequently have Sunday dinners at my grandmother's as well. I recall vividly that the pantry space we had in that home was on the back porch. A decent sized bookcase that matched my folks' bedroom set was repurposed as storage for canned goods and baking items on the porch. During a good week, there would be a few cans of soup and vegetables on the first shelf. Bad weeks, however...well, grandma would visit.

My brief experience with food insecurity from childhood has had lasting effects on me. That bookcase from the back porch now lives in my formal living room, but the pantry I've cultivated in my farmhouse is a walk-in closet lined with shelves of food suitable for a zombie apocalypse. I like buying in bulk, especially canned goods, and take tremendous pride in the order and beauty that is my well-stocked, perfectly faced, meticulously organized pantry. Oh, what's that? You need a dozen cans of reduced sodium chicken broth? Totes Magoats. Let me hook you up.

The sense of security that I achieve from my zombie apocalypse pantry reminds me of the Sunday dinners at my grandmother's. I always knew that there would be tasty food and plenty of it. Her forte was beef and homemade noodles with mashed potatoes and succotash. I have yet to master the noodles, but I'm happy to say that I now make roast beast my bitch.

zombie apocalypse pantry

81

I come from a looong line of faithful, practicing carnivores, so I learned early that a Sunday roast served with a slew of carbs is a comforting, happy thing. Going to grandma's house to eat a big slab o' flavorful meat that cooked all day is as close to a religious experience as I got as a kid. The best part of the roast is the leftover possibilities—a reincarnation if you will. Check out the recipe for the upcycled Potroastini on page 86.

roast beast

what do you mean you don't brown yours with crisco?

1 3 lb-ish chuck roast
2 TB evoo
1 TB minced garlic
1 large yellow onion, diced
1 bunch celery, sliced into veggie tray-size chunks
5 large carrots, sliced into veggie tray-size chunks
2 C beef stock or water
Kosher salt and ground pepper

Serves: 6
Pairs with: folks who identify with Norm Abram.
Consideration: plan for leftovers & save the crock liquid!

In a large pan, add the evoo and crank the heat to medium high. Throw in the onions and sauté for about 2 minutes until they start thinking about becoming translucent, then swirl them into an outer ring to make room for the bigass slab o' meat.

Plop the meat in the center of the pan and generously salt and pepper the top. Allow the meat to brown for about 5 minutes, stirring around the onions so they don't stick. Lift up the slab to check the bottom. When there's no pink left and there are a few darker brown patches, it's time to put your thang down, flip it and reverse it.

82   (continued on next page)

Add more salt and pepper on the flipped side, then throw in the garlic and give it a good stir to incorporate it into the onions. Allow the bottom side to brown about five more minutes, then flip the slab to each side and get a quality sear for about a minute.

Set your crock pot on high and get ready to chop some veg. Wash the celery and slice each stalk in half lengthwise, then into sticks about the length of your pinky (usually four segments per stalk.). Peel the carrots and cut them the same length, then cut the segments in half and in half again to make 4 chunks on the fat end. Just make sure they end up as fork-pokable sticks. Toss all the veg in the bottom of the crock.

When the roast beast is done browning, nestle it in the veg and dump the onions over the top and around the sides. Add the beef stock (water works just fine if you don't have any on hand.) Put the lid on the crock and cook for 4-6 hours on high or 8ish hours on low. The veggies will be tender AF and the chunk o' meat will be fall-apart when done.

Serve with Crack Mashed Potatoes and Easy Peasy Gravy.

Let's keep it real for a minute: I didn't learn how to make gravy until I was in my 40's. My mama made gravy when I was little using pan drippings and flour, but the finished product resembled wallpaper paste. Learning the cornstarch and broth method healed my culinarily-scarred memory of gravy. You can use this method for any type of meat or veggies cooked in the crock pot, or just grab some canned stock and go to town.

easy-peasy gravy
smother this shit on everything

2 C liquid from a crocked meat/ veggies or canned/boxed stock
3 TB corn starch
1 ½ C water
Salt and pepper

Directions

If using crock pot liquid, place two cups of it in a gravy separator. Allow to sit for a few minutes until you see the fat layer forming on the top. Dispense all but the gross top layer into a saucepan while your kid yells "huhuhuh it's peeing" and then bring the broth to a slow boil over medium high heat.

If using canned/boxed broth, just pour into pan and start the boil.

In a container with a lid (like one you'd make a shaky dressing in) add the cornstarch and water. Shake it like a polaroid picture until combined, then add it to the boiling broth. Start gently whisking. When you see bubbles forming around the edge and the liquid boiling inward, reduce the heat and continue whisking. When the gravy reaches your desired consistency (should be within 3 minutes), pull it from the heat and stir one more time. Add salt and pepper to taste.

Leslie Hart-Davidson

At a fancy schmancy restaurant one time, I was served mashed potatoes in…wait for it…a martini glass. "Charming!" I thought as I stared at this new interpretation of a classic standard side dish.

Fueled by the creativity only found after consuming several glasses of wine, I held up the potatotini and thought "Hey! I could put a whole meal in one of these!" and Potroastini was born.

¾ C leftover roast beef
2 C mashed potatoes
¾ C veg from original roast
½ C corn kernels
¾ C gravy
4+ cheese coins (recipe pg 60)
Salt and pepper to taste

Directions

Set out the martini glasses and create an assembly line to build the potroastini simultaneously and wow the crap out of your guests.

I'll gladly provide the order of operations for the layering process, but please know that this is your jam and you can build it however you want. If you want a meat-heavy version (huhuhuh TWSS), rock on. If your uterus is demanding a tatie-intensive dish, good for you. Fill the glass as high as you want with whatevs you want as many times as you want. You do you, boo. Here's the framework:

Splash of gravy
Bloop of taties
Dash of corn
Sprinkling of other veg
Splash of gravy
Heap of meat
Bloop of taties
Splash of gravy
Cheese coin nestled into taties
Salt & pepper topping

Place the potroastini on a small plate for serving with bonus cheese coins or a roll on the side.

potroastini
e'body love parfait.

Food is Love

Serves: 4
Pairs with: folks who identify with Martha Stewart.
Skill-Level: Even Sara can assemble this dish.

87

food matters because **bonding**

Ready for an "awwwww" moment? I met my future husband Bill while still in middle school. My best friend and his best friend were siblings, so we'd frequently see each other on weekends and during school breaks. I started officially dating him my freshman year of high school when he was already a junior. By the time he left for college two years later, I had grown quite fond of his mom Donna. She was (and remains to this day) a confident, funny, warm, loving person who appreciated my presence in her eldest son's life. Bonus: she's one hell of a cook.

Bill and I maintained a long-distance relationship when he was away at college, but that didn't mean that I stopped interacting with his family during those two years. Once a week, Donna would fetch me on a school night and bring me back to her house for amazing dinners and cooking lessons. It was a lovely escape from the uneasy vibe at home (my folks were mid-divorce for those years), so I enjoyed focusing on the company of Donna and the lesson that week.

Donna would teach me basic techniques, entertain me with stories, and impart a love of the process that I hadn't yet experienced. "You need to use your senses to cook well," she explained while making breakfast for dinner. "Listen to the potatoes. Hear how they're sizzling differently now? And do you smell the change yet from when you first put them in the pan? Looking doesn't tell you everything. Trust your ears and your nose more."

The skills I learned from my weekly Donna dinners translated as beautifully to life as they did to food. Cooking was just the medium for absorbing all

Food is Love

of her wisdom. I see and listen and pay attention to so much more in each situation I face in life as a direct result of Donna's lesson for fried potatoes.

Damn I love that woman.

Disco Donna and baby BHD

Want to know something funny? My mother-in-law Donna can't eat this dish because green peppers don't agree with her (and she'll gladly describe with great specificity exactly why. *Several times.*) In true Food is Love fashion, however, she gladly taught me this meal that she lovingly makes for her husband Rick because he enjoys the dish so much. The original white rice and hamburger stuffing that she shared with me decades ago has transformed into a slightly healthier version of comfort food. You can laugh at that statement when you see how much cheese is in the recipe. But hey, I tried.

2 cups cooked yellow rice
(most of an 8 oz pkg)
1 14 oz can chicken stock
1 onion, chopped
2 TB evoo
2 cooked chicken breasts
(about 2 cups)
1 14 oz can diced tomatoes
1 4 oz can chopped
green chiles
1 ½ C shredded
mozzarella cheese
Enough slices of provolone
cheese to cover each pepper
⅛ C tomato sauce
Salt and pepper to taste

Serves: 6-8
Pairs with: Tums.
Consideration: these little guys freeze well when sliced in half.

Break out the rice cooker and toss in the package of yellow rice and can of chicken stock. Stir until all of the powdery bits are dissolved, then set it to cook white rice.

Preheat the oven to 400 degrees. Grab a big pot and fill it halfway with water, then get a high simmer/low boil going while you do pepper prep.

Cut the tops off the peppers and clean out the pulpy bits and seeds. Using tongs, dip the pepper "cups" into the water so that each one is halfway filled, then arrange them so they weeble wobble but don't fall down.

(continued on next page)

three-butt peppers
are better than
four-butt peppers

The goal is to parboil the peppers so they're not raw tasting when complete, but also not cooked entirely so they lose structural integrity in the oven. About five minutes of a low boil should get them there. Set the drained peppers in a Pyrex baking dish and get ready to rumble, then rinse the pan for the next step.

Return the pan to the cooktop and add the evoo. Sautee the onion using medium high heat until translucent, about 5 minutes. While the onions are cooking, shred or dice your chicken into bite-sized chunks.

Remove pan from the heat and add the following goodies: chicken, diced tomatoes and green chiles, rice, and shredded cheese. Give it a good stir and see how much tomato sauce it needs to be stuffable into the peppers, but not too wet. About 1/8 cup should do.

Shove the filling into peppers using a teaspoon, packing firmly. Arrange the peppers in the pan so there's no danger of weebling, then pour over the remaining tomato sauce.
Bake uncovered for 25-30 minutes, then pull out the Pyrex to cover each pepper with a slice of provolone cheese. Turn the oven to broil and watch carefully as the melty, browny goodness happens. Allow the peppers to cool for about five minutes before serving.

Serve a whole pepper for a hungry person or sliced in half for a more reasonable portion. (Yeah, good luck with that.)

Food is Love

Throughout the 1980's, my husband's mother Donna worked in a Greek diner. The owner Poda, a stern immigrant, held her prized Greek salad recipe close. Despite Donna's pleas for the deets on the veggielicious side dish, Poda kept mum. Donna never did get the recipe, but she was able to reverse engineer it enough to call it good.

This salad is easy to assemble, but needs a hot minute to "come together" as the brine draws out the water from the veggies. It's magnificent as a base to top with grilled slices of steak or chicken, and tastes even better the next day.

donna's greek salad
damn woman wouldn't give me the recipe so I figured it out myself.

Salad:
3 medium cucumbers, diced
2 large tomatoes, diced
1 medium Vidalia or sweet onion, diced
1 C crumbled feta cheese in brine
1 C pitted Kalamata olives

Dressing:
⅓ C evoo
¼ C lemon juice
1 TB feta brine
2 TB Lawry's season salt
1 TB minced garlic
1 tsp dried oregano

Dice cucumbers, tomatoes and onion and place in a big bowl. Crumble the feta over the top and plop in the pitted olives, stirring gently. Whisk together the dressing goodies and pour over the veggie mix, stirring to coat. Now here's the challenging part: cover the salad and stick it in the fridge for a minimum of 3 hours to develop the dressing. I pinky swear it's worth it.

Serves: 6
Pairs with: low-key industrial espionage.
Genre: you'll be popular at summer cookouts with this offering.

94

Use this salad
in wraps, too!

My father-in-law, Fred Davidson, was an amaaaazing baker. My favorite Christmas treat of his was orange balls, a happy concoction of boozy chocolately goodness. His confections were revered regionally since he would gift and sell the goodies each holiday, and Fred was happy to pass along the knowledge and recipe to anyone who believed that food is love.

A dozen of these little bad boys stuffed in a little white bakery box tied with ribbon would make a super posh treat (says the girl who does this on the regular).

6 oz pkg Nilla Wafers
1 TB grated orange rind
6 oz pkg Pecan Sandies
1 14 oz can sweetened
condensed milk
1 ½ C finely chopped pecans
¼ C Triple Sec liquer
⅓ C sweetened cocoa
confectioner's sugar

Directions

Place the Nilla Wafers in a large plastic baggie and seal well. Smash the shit out of the cookies with a rolling pin or paillard hammer until they're fine little crumbs. Repeat with the Pecan Sandies in another bag, then pour them in a large bowl.

Add the finely chopped pecans, cocoa, orange rind and con-

densed milk. Mix well. Add in the triple sec, then pour a shot for yourself (though I recommend mixing it with vodka & juice) to toast Fred Davidson and all kind-hearted men who made the world a better place. Give the ingredients a final mix, cover, then chill it for an hour or so.

Powder your hands with confectioner's sugar like a gymnast chalks up before the parallel bars. Roll a bit of chilled dough in your hands roughly the size of a shooter marble, then plop the ball into a waiting dish of more confectioner's sugar. Scooch it around until evenly covered, then place it on parchment paper. Periodically clean off your hand and apply more sugar so the balls won't stick (TWSS).

fred's orange balls
huhuhuhuh. you said balls.

96

Yields: 8 dozen
Pairs with: holidays and lots of guests.
Consideration: pace yourself to prevent sugar tummy.

Refrigerate Fred's Orange Balls in a lid-tight container to avoid drying out.

food matters because **old traditions**

Baby gherkin pickles. Cubes of Colby cheese. Crock pots filled with bbq. Tiny cokes in glass bottles. All of these foods instantly take me back to family gatherings from my childhood. A dozen or more relatives would wander in and out of the kitchen refilling drinks, telling jokes and searching for a few more tasty morsels.

Food tastes different when it has a connection to a sentimental experience. The holiday gatherings from both sides of my family (and later my in-laws) involved special treats and tasty dishes that I enjoy replicating to this day. Cooking the "gathering foods" helps to remind me of the traditions that my relatives began generations before, and eating those dishes allows me to feel a connection to the relatives who are long gone.

When I invite folks to dinner and serve something from the "gathering food" menu, I'm quick to entertain to my guests with the origin story of the dish and any memories of the relative who created it. "These are Thelma's pinwheels," I'll explain. "She made them from leftover pie dough. Tough cookie, that Thelma. At age 87, she woke up in the middle of the night to find a strange man in her bed. She beat him with a broom until he hustled out."

Food is Love

Barb and Artie Derr
in 70's polaroid glory

Don't miss the opportunity to ask your relatives for recipes while they are still able to do so. We will never know if it was the well water or an unspoken seasoning composition that makes Grammy's soups so delicious unless we ask.

99

Christmas Eve gatherings in the 1970's at the home of my mama's older brother Artie Derr were glorious culinary times. I fondly recall the spread that he and my Aunt Barb would put out for the hungry crowd: little 8oz glass bottles of Coca Cola that my brother and I loved, appetizers for days, and the avocado green crock pot full of yummy family recipe beef bbq. To my young palette, the bbq was a delicate fight between the pungent vinegar and the sweetness of the brown sugar. I ate pounds of it as a kid, always going back for one more sandwich washed down with an icy cold fully-caffeinated, completed sugared Coke. Ahh, the 70's.

derr bbq
We are Missouri folk, but vinegar bbq is better in the crock pot.

2 lb pork roast or beef roast
2 lg onions, diced
2 TB evoo
1 C water
2 C tomato juice
¼ C vinegar
½ C ketchup
2 TB brown sugar
2 tsp dry mustard
½ tsp chili powder
2 tsp paprika
2 TB worchestershire
Salt and pepper

Serves: 6
Pairs with: a plastic dust cover for your velour sofa.
Consideration: double it for a kickass potluck party.

Heat evoo in a skillet and add the diced onion. Add salt and pepper and sauté for one minute, then move the onions to the outer ring of the pan to make room for the meat (TWSS). Place the roast in the pan and sprinkle with salt and pepper. Allow the roast to brown using medium-high heat, about 5 minutes per side.

While the roast is browning, grab a bowl and start assembling the sauce. If you don't want to dirty a bowl, just throw everything from the water down the list in the crock pot and give it a stir. When the roast is done browning, plop it along with the onions in the crock as well.

Spoon some sauce over the top of the roast and make sure it's all nestled pretty in the pot.

If you're in a hurry, cook it on high for 4-6 hours. If you have longer and throw it in the crock in the morning for dinner, set it on low. About 20 minutes before you're ready to serve, take a potato masher and go to town on the roast so it falls apart. A large fork will do the same job if you don't have the masher. The goal is to incorporate the shreds of meat with all the yummy sauce.

The most traditional way to serve Derr BBQ is on a regular sandwich bun. They make great sliders with a piece of Colby cheese as well, or you could plop a spoonful over yellow rice. If you're adventurous, check out my favorite interpretation of the dish on the next page: Ropa Vieja.

Much like Jesus turned water into wine, the lore of Ropa Vieja is a similar culinary miracle. The Spanish story is that a beggar was so famished that he shredded his own clothing to make a soup, then prayed over it for a tasty transformation. The soup became a miraculously meaty stew for his family.

The story of Ropa Vieja is over 500 years old, but it's new to my repertoire. I adapted it from the Derr bbq recipe to elevate the flavor and style of a beloved childhood dish. Ropa is a fantastic dinner item for picktastic eaters as they can customize their toppings to make a perfect meal served over rice.

The quantities of these toppings will be a little loosey goosey depending on what is preferred. You do you, boo.

ropa vieja
old clothes? i'm not eating old clothes for dinner.

Whatever leftover Derr bbq you have (pork or beef)
1 tomato, diced
1 small white or 1 bunch green onion, diced
5 radishes, sliced thin
1 bunch cilantro, chopped
Handful sliced jalapenos
Bloops of sour cream

Serves: 2ish, depending on leftovers
Pairs with: a desire to clean out the fridge.
Consideration: easy gateway to ethnic food.

Choose your own adventure!

Slice and chop and present.
Top and love and eat.

OR

For a buffet-style gathering, place individual toppings in dishes for guests to build their own. Save on dishes by using a large cutting board to present all of the indregients for plate-building.

swap out the rice for riced cauliflower to lower the carbs

Being from the Midwest, I'm contractually obligated to serve a casserole at any family gathering. The dish of choice for the Derr family gatherings was scalloped potatoes, or "cheesy taties" as I called them as a kid. I fondly recall the original incarnation of this dish that used Kraft cheese slices and a whole stick of margarine. The Exxon Valdese-style oil slick that was the hallmark top layer gave way to a more gentile version with big-girl aromatics and a little less oil as I played with the recipe over the years. I think the Derr women would approve.

5 large russet potatoes, sliced pretty thin
½ yellow onion, sliced thin
Salt and pepper
½ tsp garlic powder, divided
1 sprig rosemary
1 C whole milk
1 C heavy whipping cream
4 C sharp cheddar cheese

Directions

Preheat the oven to 425 degrees. In a saucepan, heat the milk and heavy cream with the rosemary sprig until it begins to simmer. Turn off the heat and allow it to steep for about 20 minutes while you prepare the gratin.

Coat the bottom of the Pyrex pan with a non-stick spray. Prepare the potato and onion slices by dividing them into four even piles. Lay down the first layer of potatoes, overlapping just a tiny bit. Sprinkle on salt and pepper along with 1/8 tsp of the garlic powder, then toss on the onions. Finish the layer with one cup of cheese sprinkled on evenly. Repeat for four layers, finishing with the cheese.

Remove the rosemary from the pan of dairy goodness and give it a good stir. Pour carefully and evenly over the potatoes. Cover with nonstick foil and bake for 50ish-60 minutes.

When the potatoes are fork tender, remove the foil and broil for a hot minute to get the top golden brown.

Remove and let rest for 10ish minutes if you can stand it.

Serves: 6-8
Pairs with: salty meat and saltier conversation.
Consideration: crazy good reheated for leftovers.

In Ohio, referring to "spaghetti" will net you this question: "EYE-talian or chili?" While the previous recipe for Jim Hart's meatballs and sauce falls firmly into the EYE-talian spaghetti category, my mama had a kickass recipe for chili spaghetti (or "sketti" as I called it for short). Since it's my mama's cooking, it basically involves browning meat and throwing shit in a pot. Super simple, it makes a crapton to feed a crowd on a budget and is full of flavor and love.

1 lb 90 % lean ground beef
1 medium onion, diced
3 TB evoo
1 can (46oz) tomato juice
2 14 oz cans diced tomatoes
1 15.5 oz can chili hot beans
1 15.5 oz can chili mild beans
1TB plus 1 tsp cumin
3 tsp salt
2 tsp pepper
2 tsp minced garlic
1 lb box spaghetti noodles
Parmesean cheese for garnish

Directions

In a large pot, heat evoo on medium and add the diced onion and 1 tsp of salt. Stir until translucent, then add the ground beef and 1 tsp pepper. Stir/mush/chop/pound and otherwise take out all your frustration on the meat as it browns in the pot.

Add garlic and stir.

When the ground beef ceases to be pink, dump in the cans of tomatoes, beans and juice. Add the cumin, remaining salt and pepper and stir around to combine. Reduce the heat to medium-low and simmer while the sketti cooks, stirring occasionally.

Cook the sketti according to package directions. When it's all al-dente-fied, drain and grab a plate.

To serve chili sketti Ohio style, plate a layer of sketti and place a ladle of chili on top, sauce and all. If you wish, top with shaky cheese (grated parmesan). Other serving options include a bowl of the steaming beany goodness topped with shredded cheddar cheese, jalapenos and sour cream.

chili sketti

no, not eye-talian sketti. Chili sketti.

Serves: 6+
Pairs with: the gradual but inexorable erosion of a manufacturing economy.
Consideration: freezes like a champ.

B HD's dad, Fred, was well known for this tasty dish made with sausage and cabbage. Fred whipped up this dinner frequently as it was cheap, fast and filling for kids. Bonus: it was tasty AF and allowed the kids to play fart-related games for a full day after.

1 link smoked sausage or kielbasa
1 large yellow onion, sliced
1 head green cabbage, cored and chopped into 1" pieces
1 TB evoo
1 28 oz can whole tomatoes, sliced in half
2 14 oz cans chicken or vegetable stock
1 TB kosher salt
Pepper to taste

In a dutch oven, heat the evoo on medium and add the onions. Sweat until translucent, about 3 minutes. Toss in the sausage and allow it to render until it starts to brown.
Add allll the cabbage (even though it looks like it'll overflow) along with the TB of kosher salt. Stir to coat the cabbage and allow it to cook for 15-20 minutes until it reduces by about 1/3 in volume and the white parts of the cabbage are tender.

Deglaze the pan with stock and stir in the big can of halved tomatoes. Increase the heat and bring to a fast bubbling simmer (like your intestines will be the next day) for one minute, then back off the heat to medium and cook for another 20ish minutes until the sauce thickens and the cabbage is perfectly tender.

Serves: 6
Pairs with: a fashionable Babushka while cooking.
Consideration: crazy good leftovers.

stuff
bachelors eat stuff. it's that simple.

108

Serve with
crusty bread
and butter

When my husband Bill and I married in July of 1994, we chose to have our high school drama teacher Linda Bodey officiate the non-denominational ceremony. The tone and content of the ceremony was exactly what we had requested from Bodey: radically egalitarian and quite progressive for the time. Most of our relatives shook their heads and scoffed at the lack of both Jesus & tradition during the event, but Bill and I felt comfortable with the overall message.

After the ceremony, Bodey pulled us aside to offer us gifts. "I need you to open this now so I can explain," she said. The gift box contained several Christmas decorations, including a vintage-looking Santa statue and a lovely knitted blanket with holiday theme. "I know it's July, but there's a purpose behind these," she began. "Until now, you've both lived your lives under the traditions of your individual families. YOU are a family now. It's time to start your own traditions during the holidays and beyond."

The enormity of Bodey's gift hit home during our first married Christmas when both graduate school and my new career in retail management curtailed our holiday travel home. Taking Bodey's advice, Bill and I decided to create a new family tradition and prepare a special dinner followed by a decadent breakfast the next morning. Our tradition of shrimp cocktail and French onion soup with a breakfast of French toast with strawberries was born that year and has been our favorite new tradition for decades.

ho-ho-whole lotta
new traditions

Bodey, best officiant ever,
ties the knot for BHD & LHD

111

In the mid 90's, I traveled a bunch for my corporate job and would spend a week or so in a new town training and hiring new folks. I always made friends with the dining staff at the hotel and was a creature of habit. On my third straight night of calling room service to order the crazy yummy French onion soup, my buddy said "Leslie, we know your order by now. The soup'll be up in 20 minutes." The next night, I asked for the recipe.

Each Christmas, I make this for our family dinner and serve it with shrimp cocktail.

french onion soup
shocker...she wants soup AGAIN.

2 large Vidalia onions, sliced about ½" wide
1 TB kosher salt
Fresh ground pepper
¾ stick butter
3 C reduced sodium beef stock
1 ¾ C reduced sodium chicken stock
1 TB Worcestershire
1 tsp horseradish
1 tsp minced garlic
Fresh baguette, sliced into ¼" pieces and toasted
Provolone cheese slices, 3 per bowl

In a large pot, melt the decadent chunk of butter over medium heat and add in the onion slivers. Sprinkle the salt and grind some fresh pepper until your hands are tired, then stir the little guys until the melted butter covers the onions evenly.

(continued on next page)

Serves: 4
Pairs with: someone who won't mind all the farting.
Consideration: go for the extra cheese.

it's totally ok to fight over the peeled bits of cheese on the side

113

Leslie Hart-Davidson

Whack the onions gently to separate the layers, then give it a good mix. If you like it, put a lid a on it (cue Beyoncé).

After 4ish minutes, lift the lid and stir the pretty onions, scraping up any browned bits on the bottom of the pan. Return the lid for another 4ish minutes.

When the onions are all goldeny brown, add both the stocks and stir. Start splooshing the Worcestershire, horseradish and garlic and mix it in nicely. Allow the soup to come to a boil, then reduce the heat and simmer for about 10 minutes.

Toast the baguette pieces (use tongs to prevent the tiny slices from getting caught) and set aside.

Prepare a baking sheet covered in non-stick foil or parchment for the individual serving crocks. Ladle spoonfuls of even onion-to-broth ratio about ¾ of the way into oven-safe crocks. Break the baguette slices into little chunks and sprinkle evenly over the soup. Top with a single slice of provolone. If you're a big fan of cheese, take 2-3 more slices and drape them over the sides of the crock to get the best melty goodness. Place under the broiler under high heat until GBD, about 2 minutes.

Use silicone oven mitts to remove the crock and pool of cheese to a serving plate.

In the early 80's, my family took a turn hosting the extended family Christmas gathering. My dad put me in charge of the cocktail sauce for the shrimp platter and trusted me to follow his loosey-goosey instructions of dashes and blops and sploops that I had witnessed so many times before. My aunt heard that I had whipped up the condiment and pressed me for the recipe. Not knowing that Jim Hart's recipe language was rhetorical and highly specialized, I earnestly described a Greg-sized blop of ketchup, three hip-shakes of salt, and a ball-crushing squeeze of lemon before my poor aunt turned red and said "I'll just ask your dad!"

5 TB Ketchup
¼ tsp salt
¼ tsp pepper
2 tsp worcestershire sauce
¼ tsp Tabasco
2 tsp horseradish
1 tsp lemon juice

Yeah, you can't really mess this up other than dropping lemon seeds in the dish. It's not cool to accidentally choke the folks you're feeding, so be careful with the lemon squeezing. Just mix this all together and set it out with a spoon for folks to scoop a bit for their own sea critters. If you want to be super fancy, cut some lemon wedges to place on the serving platter with the shrimp.

cocktail sauce
my hips don't lie.

Serves: 4
Pairs with: a Don Draper-style soirée.
Consideration: heavy-hand the Tabasco for hotter sauce.

The term "salad" in Ohio is wiiiiide open to interpretation. My mama's version of an everyday salad involved iceberg lettuce with a dressing made from mayo and ketchup. Waldorf was a fancy version of salad that she served with some beef dishes. I added everything beyond the apples later when a roommate made fun of me for just having mayo-d apples.

waldorf salad
well, it's a step up from iceberg and mayo.

2 large Honeycrisp, Fuji or Gala apples, chopped into bite-sized pieces with skin still on
2 stalks celery, diced
1 C green or red grapes, halved
⅓ C walnuts, chopped
¼ C Hellman's mayonnaise

Toss the apples, celery, grapes and walnuts into a large bowl. Add the bloop of mayo and gently mix everything together.

Serves: 6
Pairs with: your blue-haired aunt who keeps tissue balled up in her sleeve.
Pro Tip: No Miracle Whip.

Food is Love

use seedless grapes
so you don't wreck
your aunt's dentures

When my college intern Becca was little, she and her family celebrated Thanksgiving at her paternal Grandmother Joanne Meyer's home. Grandma made corn crunchy as a side dish until she suffered a stroke. To honor her Grandma, Becca began making the dish more frequently. This comforting, carbalicious dish is now in regular rotation with her college friends and luckily in my food world too. You shouldn't reserve something that tasty for only one day a year, so crunch on.

corn crunchy
carby side dishes are the truest form of love.

1 15 oz can regular sweet corn, drained 75%
2 15 oz cans creamed corn
1 stick unsalted butter, melted
1 16 oz tub sour cream
1 15 oz box Krusteez honey cornbread muffin mix
1 ½ tsp garlic powder
1 ½ tsp onion powder
1 ½ tsp Lawry's season salt

Preheat the oven to 350 degrees. In a large bowl, mix the items in the order listed. Pour into a 9" x 13" Pyrex pan and place in the oven for 50-60 minutes until the top is golden brown and a toothpick inserted in the center comes out clean. Allow to cool for 15ish minutes, then serve in little squares.

Serves: 6ish
Pairs with: hug from grandma.
Consideration: swap 2 ears of fresh corn or 1 ½ C frozen corn for the can.

Food is Love

Krusteez
makes a gluten
free version of
cornbread mix

Splatters, rips, wrinkles, smudges. These are the hallmarks of the hand written recipe cards I've collected from all the relatives who have passed on. I'm sad to have lost so many loved ones, but thrilled that I honor their memory by making the delightful dishes that they handed down to me so many years ago. The sucky thing is that I can't call them up and say "now tell me again how you do this part" or "can I substitute such-and-such for this dish?" It's okay, though. I've had to get creative and reinterpret some dishes, but I always feel a connection to my family as I bring out the well-worn recipe cards and get busy in the kitchen.

The connection I feel isn't just for the immediate family; it's the centuries of ancestors who shared their culture and food, passing it down for the next generation. Quite a few recipes from my mama's people are German, so I wasn't surprised to find after a thorough genealogical search that about six generations back, my super-duper-great grandfather Johan Phillip Wentz, born in 1710 in Rheinland-Pfalz, Germany set sail for America. He arrived around 1743 in Baltimore harbor, earning a spot in the family lore as a crusty one-legged sea captain.

Hand-written recipe cards are a form of art. Add a little nostalgia by creating decor through your favorite recipe cards. Framing, printing on stretched canvas and making a collage are all great ways to display meaningful decor.

MIX LIKE CRAZY YOU'RE DONE - COOK IT

100 years' worth of food knowlege

Both food and life advice hung for all to see

123

Leslie Hart-Davidson

As a kid, I recall eating my first non-Derr pumpkin pie at a restaurant. Repulsed by the bland, undercooked taste, I spit it out on my plate and horrified my entire family. Well, except my brother. He had neatly hidden his in a napkin a few minutes earlier and showed me beneath the table. "You gotta be subtle getting rid of this turd," he encouraged me. "This definitely isn't Grandma's pie."

The Derr version of pumpkin pie requires a palette that appreciates a decent level of spices. If you're a wuss and can't handle flavor (or have to cook for those peeps) then consider halving the spice amounts listed. Thelma will cry a little bit, but, ya know, food is love.

derr pumpkin pie
the spice must flow.

1 15 oz can pumpkin
2 eggs
¾ C brown sugar
½ tsp salt
3 tsp cinnamon
1 ½ tsp ginger
1 tsp cloves
1 12 oz can evaporated milk
Pie dough (rock on, Pillsbury)

Preheat the oven to 425 degrees. In a large bowl, crack the two eggs and whippy dippy. Add the pumpkin and whisk until blended. Toss in the brown sugar and spices, then mix again until combined. Finally, pour in the evaporated milk and gently mix until all the goodness comes together.

Line a 9" pie pan (I like glass) with the pie dough and do the cute pinchy thing around the edges if you're inclined. Pour in the mixture and place in center of the oven for 15 minutes. Reduce to 350 degrees and bake an additional 40-50 minutes until the top is a consistent color and an inserted butter knife comes out clean.

Yields: standard 9" pie
Pairs with: slippers, loose sweatpants and that fork you keep in your bedroom "just in case."

Wilton makes a cool 6-cavity mini pie pan that equals the guts of a 9" pie.

In the 70's, my dad loved to watch football on Sundays in the basement rec room. While I didn't really have any interest in the game, I had significant interest in the snacks that went along with it. Sitting on the scratchy Early American sofa with a pink Tupperware bowl in my lap, I'd devour the beef dip with celery stalks and green pepper slices under the watchful gaze of the scantily clad Farrah Fawcett poster. Good times.

4 oz Neufchatel cream cheese (half a standard 8oz pkg)
1 C mayo
½ small yellow onion, diced wicked fine
1 beef bouillon cube
2 TB super hot water
2 tsp Worcestershire sauce

In a small dish or prep bowl, pour the water over the bouillon cube. While the salt bomb is dissolving, grab a large bowl with high sides and plop in the cream cheese and mayo. Beat with a hand mixer until fluffy, about 2 minutes. Add the dissolved bouillon, onion and Worcestershire. Beat once more to combine.

Serve with celery sticks, green pepper slices or crackers.

Serves: 6
Pairs with: sports jerseys.
Consideration: don't substitute regular cream cheese - softer is better.

Note: If you double the recipe for a party-sized quantity, use 2 bouillon cubes BUT ONLY 3 TB water, not 4.

Food is Love

It wasn't until high school that I realized our family tradition of eating pork and sauerkraut on New Year's Day to bring luck wasn't a widely shared custom. "Get enough peas on the first?" one friend asked me. "Whu? You mean kraut?" "Black-eyed peas and greens!" she said. We both looked at each other for a minute until we traded stories of traditional food our families served for holidays. Even though my folks only served this meal on New Year's Day, I happily make it throughout the fall and winter. Hey, we can all use a little more luck.

pork and kraut
it stinks, but we need all the luck we can get.

1 ½ish lb pork tenderloin or pork loin chunk
1 32 oz jar polish sauerkraut
1 small onion, diced
¾ C chicken stock
2 TB evoo
Salt and pepper

Directions

In a nonstick pan over medium heat, add the evoo and sweat the onion with 1 tsp salt for about 2 minutes. Stir the onions around and push them to an outer ring in the pan. Plop the pork loin in the center of the pan and sprinkle with salt and pepper. Cook for about 5 minutes until the bottom side browns, then flip the pork slab and repeat the salt and pepper sprinkling. Continue stirring the onions so they don't get too brown. When the other side is a pretty brown, turn off the heat and prepare the crock pot.

Grab the crock and set it on high for 5ish hours or low for 8ish hours. Drain the kraut and plop it in the crock, using a fork to evenly distribute across the bottom. Nestle the pork chunk on the kraut, then dump the onions over the top. Add the stock around the kraut and put a lid on it.

Note: if you're using a pork loin instead of tenderloin, there will be a layer of fat on one side of the roast. Keep it on while browning and cooking to add flavor, but scrape it off before serving.

Serves: 6
Pairs with: Reader's Digest large-print edition & crack mashed taties.
Consideration: legit leftovers.

Help me settle a 30+ year-long baking battle, please. My grandmother Thelma was born in 1904. Since her mama Lulu Franklin was claimed by tuberculosis just after giving birth to her, Thelma's German stepmother Hattie raised her with tons of great recipes and a sense of both proficiency and economy in the kitchen.

My husband's grandmother Mamie was born in 1918 and grew up "not too far removed from the hills." Mamie worked as a baker at the tuberculosis hospital where she made pies by the dozen for the ailing residents daily, so saying she knew kitchen proficiency is an understatement.

The premise of these tasty treats is to use up the leftover pie dough from the day's baking and turn them into little bite-sized bits of sweet happiness filled with butter, cinnamon and sugar. Here's the battle: Thelma always referred to them as pinwheels. Mamie always referred to them as cinnamon rolls. Call them whatever you want (cough *pinwheels*) because they're delicious. Pinwheels. There, I'm done.

1 prepackaged pie dough or a large ball of leftover homemade dough
4 TB butter (half stick), melted
1 tsp sugar, plus a bit more for sprinkling
1 tsp cinnamon

Yields: 24 pinwheels
Pairs with: argumentative people.
Consideration: package a dozen for a sweet little gift.

Preheat the oven to 375 degrees. Prepare a baking sheet with parchment or non-stick foil and smush or roll out the dough into a rectangle-ish shape.

Brush most of the melted butter over the entire crust, reserving about a quarter or less for the top after rolling.

(continued on next page)

Sprinkle the cinnamon and sugar evenly over the top. Begin rolling snugly along the longest edge, making a snake-like roll. Using a sharp knife, slice the tasty snake into about ½" sections (like ready-made sugar cookies) and let them fall on the baking sheet. When all the slices are cut, give them a little space and brush each one with the remaining melted butter. Feel free to sprinkle a bit more sugar over the top if it floats your boat.

Bake for 10-12 minutes until GBD. Allow to cool for several minutes before you stuff your face with the cinnamony pinwheel goodness.

Food is Love

Mamie offers up
tasty treats

Clark County TB hospital,
circa 1910

133

Leslie Hart-Davidson

Having moved away from home immediately after graduating high school, my husband and I discovered early in our marriage that if we wanted family dinners, we'd have to drive at least 4 hours to experience them. When we had our fill of hometown family dinners filled with chain smoking and regret, we'd look instead to our local friends to invite to "family" dinners. What are friends you feed if not the family you choose? These dinners were always filled with love and laughter and venting and companionship without a hint of guilt or drama or emphysema.

mason jar bouquets are a casual but beautiful THING

Entertaining Tips

Do as much prep work as possible before guests arrive
Dinner guests want to spend time with you, not watch you toil in the kitchen.

Rock a meal in your wheelhouse
The time to experiment with a new recipe is *not* when the pressure is high.

Set the table early
Mindfully choose your plates, napkins and centerpiece before guests arrive, to free up your time for cooking.

Consider the ambience
Fire up a dinner playlist on your smart speaker, dim the lights and ensure the dining area is a comfortable temperature.

Don't overthink it
You're not Martha Stewart, so just be as human as possible and your guests will have a delightful time.

Leslie Hart-Davidson

One of my favorite things about quiche is its versatility. Need a brunchy thing to serve a bunch of people? Quiche! Need a meal planning idea for the week's lunches? Quiche! A spring dinner? QUICHE.

The versatility doesn't stop with the meal times. The incarnations of ingredients are long and lovely. This broccoli cheese version is my favorite style of egg pie, but ham, asparagus and swiss is also a favorite. Bacon and tomato quiche is amazing with an iceburg lettuce side salad. Hooray egg pie!

quiche
you don't spell it, son. you eat it!

1 slab o' dough for 9" pie
2 small broccoli crowns, cut into bite-sized chunks
2 roma tomatoes, sliced
8 oz mushrooms, thinly sliced
3 TB evoo
2 C shredded cheddar cheese, divided
3 eggs, beaten
1 C 2% milk
1 TB flour
1 tsp salt
1 tsp pepper
¼ C chicken stock

Yields: standard 9" pie
Pairs with: fans of John Hughes movies.
Considerations: reheats well when cut into chunks.

Preheat the oven to 375 degrees. Line a 9" pie pan (I like glass) with the pie dough and do the cute pinchy thing around the edges if you're inclined. Bake for 10ish minutes until the bottom is slightly brown. While cooling, evenly sprinkle ¼ cup of the cheddar cheese to bottom of the pie crust.

Cut the broccoli crowns into bite-sized chunks and place them in a microwave safe dish. Fill the dish partway with water and place plastic wrap on top. Microwave for 3ish minutes to steam the baby trees, then drain.

(continue on next page)

substitute any veg/
meat/cheese combo
for a delicious quiche

Heat the evoo in a skillet on medium heat and add the drained broccoli. Scooch the baby trees around for about 2 minutes until softened, then add the mushrooms. Sauté until slightly brown, then add the chicken stock and reduce the heat to medium low. Cook until the stock evaporates, then remove from heat.

In a large bowl, crack the three eggs and whippy dippy. Add the milk, melted butter, salt and pepper and flour. Whisk until blended. Stir in the remaining ¾ C cheddar cheese.

Place the sautéed goodies in the pie shell, leaving spaces between the trees and fungus to nestle the sliced tomatoes (don't overfill). Pour the liquid bits over the top, nudging the shredded cheese to evenly cover the top.

Place in center of the oven. Bake for 35-45 minutes until the top is a consistent color and an inserted butter knife comes out clean. Let cool for 15 minutes before serving.

138

Hierarchy of Help

The kitchen is a sacred space to some, but an afterthought to others. When you're invited to dinner at someone's home, asking the host how you can help is a nice thing to do. The host's relationship to their own kitchen will determine the type of task you're assigned.

I'm super judgey about the skill level of others offering help in my kitchen, so I have a hierarchy of tasks that I'll assign if I need help and it's offered based on the skill level of the guest. Sometimes the best thing folks can do is sit and keep me company while I cook if I don't have any tasks for them.

Here's a list of tasks that could be assigned when asked how a guest can help:

Foodie Peer: Full kitchen privileges, including accepting advice from them regarding the technique, flavor and presentation of food.

Decent Cook: Mind a dish on the stove by stirring or adding ingredients.

Novice Cook: Complete prep work including chopping and peeling.

Inexperienced Cook: Fetch items from fridge or pantry and assist with cleanup.

Can't Boil Water: Chat with the cook, set the table, pour beverages, open wine.

Leslie Hart-Davidson

One of the many, many reasons that I love my bestie Spice (her real name is Cathy Spicer, but we call each other dearie) is that she forces me out of my culinary comfort zone. When I have writing retreats with her at Casa Cohassett, she'll put food in front of me with a motherly "oh you're going to try this" glare that I am compelled to obey. Olives, funky cheeses and lamb are all on the list of things I now enjoy thanks to her prodding. The other thing on the list: Dearie Curry.

The funky fish sauce and curry paste in this recipe made my right eyebrow raise pretty damn high the first time I encountered it, but it's so delicious that it's in regular rotation at the Compound. Even my picky-ish business manager Jen requests it monthly.

dearie curry
fish sauce smells like ass.

Ingredients

4 tsp evoo
1 C chopped yellow onion (large onion)
2 tsp minced ginger
1 ½ C snow peas
1 lb protein (options: boneless skinless chicken thighs or tenders cut into bite-sized chunks, tofu cubes, or medium sized peeled & deveined raw shrimp

1 13.6 oz can coconut milk
1 TB green curry paste (Thai Kitchen sells it in a little jar)
4 TB fresh basil chiffonade
½ bunch fresh cilantro, chopped
2 TB fish sauce (trust me, even though it smells like armpits it's worth it)
2 cloves minced garlic (I highly recommend the bigass minced jar)
1 tsp turmeric
1 red bell pepper, thinly sliced

Serves: 4
Pairs with: podcast discussion.
Considerations: No meat? No problem! The vegan version is just as good!

(directions on next page)

140

chiffonade 101:
stack the leaves,
roll them tight
and slice into
thin little strips

Directions

In a bigass pan, over medium high heat, sauté onion and 1 tsp of the minced ginger in the evoo until they start to look pretty and translucent. Add the protein and mix according to this guide:

Chicken—fling it around like Samsonite luggage. You can't hurt it. Sauté until no longer pink in the middle, then pick out the chickity chunks and remove to a plate.

Tofu—press the block and reduce the moisture first, then delicately and lovingly place the protein chunks in the pan. Don't look directly at them or they'll fall apart like a hormonal teenage girl at prom whose date just made out with that bitch Becky. Coat the protein chunks as you GENTLY stir, then remove them to a plate.

Shrimp—if frozen, parboil the tasty sea critters in a seperate pan of water to get the majority of cooking done, then toss them in the pan. Stir them around for about 2 minutes and remove to a plate. If thawed, skip the parboiling.

Time to get fragrant! First, grab a whisk and stir the can of coconut milk. Zero worries if the milk comes out in chunks—just whisk that shit out. Add the curry paste, remaining ginger, garlic, fish sauce, and turmeric. Boil until thickened (about 2 minutes), then add ½ of the basil and all of the cilantro, snow peas and red pepper. Stir and let simmer for two minutes, then add your protein back. Garnish with remaining basil and serve over jasmine rice.

birth of book 2
on Spice's porch

the porch of Casa
Cohassett, where food
magically appears

Leslie Hart-Davidson

When I lived in upstate New York in the early 2000s, there were often dinners with friends at a downtown Albany restaurant called Clayton's. Their Caribbean menu featured jerk, one of my favorites dishes. I endured the relentless heat of the spice (because wuss), but wished for a tamer version I could make at home. My friend Kellie came through for me and I've been enjoying the recipe ever since. Feel free to crank up the spice level if you're into that. I appreciate my esophagus, sooooo I'll stick to the lower heat.

jerk chicken
looks like swamp ass to me.

8 boneless, skinless chicken thighs
2 yellow onions, finely chopped
1 C chopped green onion
2 TB fresh thyme
(leaves removed from the stem)
2 tsp salt
1 ½ TB sugar
2 tsp allspice
1 tsp nutmeg
1 tsp cinnamon
1 diced jalapeno pepper (double for more heat, or use a serrano)
2 tsp black pepper
2 ½ TB soy sauce
2 tsp vegetable oil
2 tsp cider or white vinegar

Sauce Directions:

You have two options for bringing together the jerk sauce, but you have no option to prevent crying during onion cutting.

Option 1: Plop all the ingredients in a high-sided bowl and use an immersion blender to buzz it to a fine consistency (not gonna lie, it looks like spinach baby poop).

Option 2: Throw everything in a blender or food processor until - you guessed it - baby poop consistency.

Serves: 6
Pairs with: one love.
Considerations: Rice and cooling salad are fabulous side dishes.

Food is Love

Crockpot Directions:

Set the crockpot to low for 8 hours or high for 4 hours. Place the chicken in the bottom and smother it all with the mixture, tossing the thighs to coat. Mix it up a bit while cooking to make sure it heats evenly, but don't mush them to oblivion. A recognizable piece of chicken is what you're after here.

Note: Thighs are the best since they don't dry out like breasts.

Oven Directions:

Preheat the oven to 400 degrees. Place the chicken thighs in a Pyrex baking pan and smother them with the jerk sauce, making sure the chicken is evenly coated. Bake uncovered for 30-40ish minutes until chicken is no longer pink inside.

Fun fact: dairy has been cooling the tongues of the capsaicin-afflicted for 8,000 years. The casein proteins in milk break down the heat bits of chili oils, relieving the pain from spicy foods. This yogurt-based cooling salad is a take on Indian raita, which serves a similar purpose. It's the chunky uncle of condiments and a must-have for spicy jerk.

cooling salad
mint and dairy? seriously?

2 medium English cucumbers (the long skinny dudes), chopped
3 roma tomatoes, relieved of their inner goo (chopped and seeded)
¼ C mint leaves or one of the little plastic containers from the grocery
1 C plain Greek yogurt
Salt and pepper to taste

Throw the cukes and tomatoes in a big bowl. Prepare the mint by removing the leaves from the stems since the stems are woody mofos. Add the mint and yogurt to the bowl, then stir. Finish with salt and pepper to taste.

Greek yogurt is wicked high in protein, so cooling salad could easily be a stand alone dinner.

Yields: 3ish cups
Pairs with: Karens who need to see the manager because she doesn't do SPICY.
Consideration: tasty with grilled meats.

Cooling salad gets too watery in the fridge, so use it or lose it

If your memory of Thanksgiving cranberries is similar to mine, I bet you're thinking of bopping the table to make the cylindrical mass with concentric lines from the metal can jiggle on its serving platter. "Make it dance again!" I'd tell my brother as the adults would yell at us to shush.

Cranberries don't have to be the sad, gelatinous Pixar character of our childhood. I'd like to give you a new, more grown-up version of the tart turkey condiment: boozy cranberries. These beauties are so next-level that they make hipsters weep with joy. They aren't even reserved for Thanksgiving! You can use it as spread on artisan breads, a topping for pancakes, or a compote over a block of soft cheese for a bougie party. Any way you use them, they're SO. DAMN. GOOD.

boozy cranberries
do you have to let it linger?

1 12oz package whole cranberries (not dried. Frozen is okay, but thaw before using)
1 C sugar
1 C water
Zest of 1 orange
1 shot Triple Sec

In a small pan, dissolve the sugar in water over medium heat to make simple syrup, stirring occasionally. When the syrup begins bubbling, plop in the cranberries and turn up the heat until they boil. Back it off to prevent spillover and continue to cook for 5ish minutes over medium heat until the berries burst open.

Remove the pan from the heat and add the zest of one orange and one shot of triple sec. Mix, then cover and allow to sit at room temperature for an hour. Serve chilled.

Yields: about 2 cups
Pairs with: a merit badge for adulting.
Considerations: no wrong time of year to enjoy these.

148

Food is Love

Buy extra bags of
cranberries in
November to freeze
for year round use

Before starting my own company, I spent 10 years being a manager for four different retail corporations. My superpower as a leader was always in community building and bringing teams together to work for a common goal (even when that goal was sometimes to get an evil, douchy boss fired decades before #metoo). Much of the team building and bonding revolved around a common love: food. I'd frequently bring in goodies from home just for the hell of it, bake yummy treats around the holidays, and arrange for themed pot lucks during lunch breaks. Recipes for the yummy dishes were always shared, and it gave the staff a reason to chat with each other on a topic that didn't involve work. Teams work better when well fed, and it's a tradition that I continue with my design staff at HDD Studios to this day.

Best Pot Luck Recipes for Work Place Events
1. Party Ball
2. Corn Crunchy
3. Derr BBQ
4. Hashbrown Casserole

enough plates to feed
the HDD Studios army

FUCK
YEAH

when co-workers let you
know how they really feel

151

Leslie Hart-Davidson

One of my coworkers once brought in a soup to share during our Soup-er-bowl party. Charlene wasn't an…uhhh… *experienced* cook, so she tried to recreate a corn chowder without the recipe that her mom had used years before.

The result was a can of corn floating in milk with a few raw potatoes in it. "I just nuked it and stirred it around. I like it though!" she said.

Food is love, so we all thanked her for the inspiration. I started playing around with the idea of a corn and potato type soup and ended up making this one-pot concoction that's as simple as dumping a shit-ton of cans in a pot and stirring. I promise it's not floating in milk.

corn chowdaaahhh
ten tin cans tend to tempt you.

½ stick butter
1 yellow onion, diced
1 tsp kosher salt
1 tsp black pepper
4 small Yukon gold taties, diced
1 green bell pepper, diced (three butted variety)
1 15 oz can chicken stock
2 tsp dried basil
2 15 oz cans cream corn
2 15 oz cans whole kernel sweet corn
1 28 oz can crushed tomatoes
1 15 oz can diced tomatoes
1 4 oz can diced green chiles
¼ C heavy whipping cream
2 C shredded cheddar cheese
Sour cream and fresh basil for garnish, if desired

In a large pot over medium heat, add the butter and onion and season with the salt and pepper. Sauté and stir a few times until translucent, about 4 minutes. Add the diced Yukon taties, stirring to remove any stuck bits of the onion. Add the chicken stock and basil, then turn the heat to medium high. Don't worry if the liquid doesn't submerge the taties—they just need to soften a bit before the remaining ingredients are added.

When the taties are mostly fork tender (about 10 minutes), add the green pepper and allll the cans of stuff. Turn down the heat to medium and give everything a good stir.

152

Allow the chowder to lightly bubble for about 12 minutes, turning down the heat if necessary to prevent a big boil.

Finally, add the cheese ½ cup at a time, folding it in like Moira Rose instructed David. (If you don't watch *Schitt's Creek*, you're missing out. Just stir it.) Add the heavy whipping cream and give it a final swish.

Serve with a dollop of sour cream and a leaf of fresh basil if you're feeling fancy.

Yields: 6
Pairs with: a thick east-coast accent.
Consideration: don't let the veggies fool you--this is not a healthy meal.

Mary Hart would frequently make party ball for potluck gatherings at work because the ingredients were wicked cheap and it made enough to feed a crowd. I recall vividly how mama snorted and laughed when a coworker tried her party ball for the first time on a potluck day. "It's so fancy!" the coworker commented. Mama choked on her Triscuit and smiled graciously. "Ah, yes" mama replied. "Nothin' but the best for you, Clark." The coworker missed the National Lampoon's reference, but gladly ate more.

mama's party ball
yeahhhh, it's a party in my mouth.

1 8oz package Neufchatel cream cheese
1 2oz package Buddig chipped beef, chopped
1 bunch green onion, diced
1 TB Worcestershire sauce

In a high-sided bowl, plop in all the ingredients. Use a hand mixer on low to combine everything, slowly increasing the speed until the mixture comes together. The glob might get trapped in the beaters, so be sure to unplug the mixer before shoving a knife or narrow spatula between the beater to free it. Scrape the sides of the bowl with a large spoon, forming the mixture into a ball. Plop on a plate and surround with Triscuits or other harder crackers.

Yields: one softball-sized sphere that serves 6.
Pairs with: inappropriate comments and questionable humor.

Food is Love

The appetizer game is strong with intern Becca. These tasty fried veggie nuggets blew me away the first time she made them at the Compound, prompting me to ask what other culinary masterpieces she was hiding from me.

I guarantee you'll be thrilled with the taste and texture of these delightful chicken wing substitutes. If you're looking for a vegan version, swap the eggs for coconut milk.

one head of cauliflower, chopped into golf ball-sized chunks

Sauce
¼ C soy sauce
½ C sweet chili sauce
2 TB Frank's hot sauce
1 TB brown sugar
2 tsp water

Coating
2 C regular or GF flour
3 eggs, beaten
1 tsp garlic powder
1 tsp onion powder
1 tsp chili powder
1 tsp black pepper
1 tsp Lawry's season salt
1 tsp cayenne pepper
½ tsp cinnamon
48oz vegetable oil for frying

In a large frying pan, pour in 2 inches of vegetable oil (ensuring that at least an inch is left before the top of the pan)and heat to 350 degrees. Test a tiny piece of the cauliflower by tossing it in the oil to ensure it bubbles and bobs rather than splats and sinks.

Create the sauce by whisking all of the ingredients in a bowl, then set aside.

While the oil is heating, put together the dredge by mixing the dry ingredients with a fork in a wide-mouthed bowl, combining well. In another bowl, beat the eggs.

(continued on next page)

make a main course "steak" from the same technique using a large lateral slice of cauliflower

Serves: 4-6
Pairs with: blue cheese dressing or hot sauce.
Consideration: Frying novices can try this recipe without the risk of undercooking meat.

Create a dredge station by lining up the bowl of beaten eggs, then the flour dredge, then a sheet of wax paper or parchment for placing the cauliflower bits before frying.

Cut the cauliflower head into small bite-sized pieces and place in a colander for a rinse. Shake off any excess water, then dip each brain-looking chunk first into the eggs, then immediately into the flour dredge for a good toss. When the brain bit is coated evenly, place it on the paper and move on to the next.

It's fry time! Be sure to have a paper towel-lined plate next to the fry station and commit to being in front of the stove for the next 15 minutes. The first rule of frying is that you DON'T WALK AWAY FROM FRYING FOOD.

Channel your inner frycook SpongeBob and use tongs to drop the brain bits into the oil in a clockwise pattern starting at six closest to you and working around in concentric rings, being careful not to crowd the pan. After about one minute, use tongs or a slotted spatularrrr to flip the cauliflower in the same order they were placed so they fry evenly. The brain bits are done when the coating is GBD, about 3 minutes.

GBD: golden, brown and delicious

Remove the cauliflower bits to the paper towel, then repeat the process in batches until all the little veggie bits are fried. When the batches are complete, pop the bits into a large bowl and pour the sauce over the top, stirring to combine. Serve with a side of hot sauce or blue cheese dressing.

Eating Away From Home

When I started at Michigan State, I quickly realized that routine meals were a luxury and I had taken for granted the familiarity of seeing the same faces around the table everyday. I spent most of my meals freshman year meandering around Brody caf by myself, content to post up in a booth and watch Netflix on my laptop. But when I moved off campus and found a solid group of friends and a mentor, cooking together became a regular thing. The comfort of having a family away from home to unwind and share a meal with was undoubtedly a lifesaver at times. If I could offer one piece of advice to anyone who is new to eating away from home, it would be to find your Food Family. Seek out people you can grab dinner with; at home, at a restaurant, or even virtually (thanks Covid!). The joy of sharing a meal with familiar faces is soothing to soul and further proof that Food is Love.

Contributed by HDD Studios intern, Becca Meyer

Leslie Hart-Davidson

food matters because **gifting**

After about 10 years together, my husband Bill and I stopped exchanging traditional gifts for birthdays and Christmas. Instead, we focused more on experiences and food. The Birthday Challenge was instituted long ago and has created some of the most incredible meals we've ever had. It's not just a one-off though; it's an opportunity to hone a cooking skill that keeps giving. Here's the deal: the birthday person challenges the other with either a specific meal or a technique. The first Birthday Challenge from Bill was fried chicken. I had never fried anything in my life, so it took some significant research and practice to get it right. To this day, fried chicken remains one of our favorite meals because of the story of the challenge, the significant effort it took to perfect it, and because fucking delicious.

Other Birthday Challenges have included next-level mac & cheese (see pg 234), eggs benedict with hollandaise sauce, fish tacos, and cake from scratch. The idea of gifting food is catching on with our family as well; my mother-in-law would rather I cook for her than take her out to eat, and my brother preferred Jim Hart's meatballs and sauce over anything I could buy him.

Birthday Challenge List

Fried Chicken	Learning to fry...and I ain't got wings...(cue Tom Petty)
Fajita Feast	Filet mignon seriously leveled up the meal
Apple Chimi Cheesecake	Reverse engineered Applebee's recipe for the win!
Sweet Corn Chicken Soup	Copycat recipe from our college-era chinese restaurant
Shrimp Scampi & Cheddar Bay Biscuits	The era of not having to go "out" to have a great meal
Eggs Blackstone	Mastering the mother sauces! Bechamel was a winner.
Panang Curry	Oh, hello new spices from the Asian market.
Naan	Yay for pre-Pandemic versitile dough making!
Beef Pho	Tons of local pho retaurants made this a must-have.
Fish Tacos	California food truck fare inspired by a Rick Bayless recipe.
Puttanesca	Ree Drummond's recipe totally won me over.
Mussels	Axed from the Jolly Pumpkin menu, but revived for my birthday.

Leslie Hart-Davidson

These grown-up Hot Pockets are perfect for an easy dinner or large gathering. They'd even rock as a lunch item since you can walk around with their neat packaging like a boss. "What's in your Hot Pocket?" you'll be asked. "Happiness. Happiness is in my Hot Pocket."

are you hungry? would you like a hot pocket?

1 lb fresh chorizo
2 russet potatoes
1 14 oz can chicken stock
3 TB evoo
2 TB tomato paste
2 tsp cumin
1 tsp oregano
1 tsp basil
3 TB minced garlic
1 green bell pepper, chopped
1 large onion, chopped
1 4 oz can diced green chiles
1 egg
1 TB milk
3 TB water
3 boxes of Pillsbury pie crust (6 total)
salt & pepper

Yields: 24 medium pockets.
Pairs with: plenty of counter-space.
Consideration: Freeze half the goo in a ziploc bag for later.

Dice the russet potatoes. Bring ¾ can of chicken stock to a boil in a small pan and cook the diced potatoes for about 5 minutes until fork stabbable, but not completely cooked. Drain and set aside.

In a large skillet, heat the evoo and add onion, bell pepper and salt & pepper to taste. When the onions become translucent, add the garlic, chiles, tomato paste, basil, oregano and cumin. Stir and add a TB or so of the reserved chicken stock as needed so the mixture isn't pasty.

Add the chorizo to the pan and take out all of your frustration on the block of spiced porky goodness by hacking/crumbling or otherwise breaking up the meat and stirring it around the mixture until cooked through. Throw in the potatoes and the remaining chicken

162

(continued on next page)

163

164

Food is Love

stock, then simmer until the mixture is a consistency that won't make the dough gooey but isn't hella-dry either. Remove from heat and let it come to room temp or shove it in the freezer for a couple minutes while you prepare the dough.

Dough time! Preheat the oven to 400 degrees. Prepare two cookie sheets with parchment or non-stick foil. In a ramekin, whisk the egg and milk and set aside. Grab another ramekin and fill with a few TB of water.

Unwrap one of the dough sleeves (you can totes use your own dough, btw. Knock yourself out!) and place on a flat surface. Using a 2-cup Pyrex prep bowl turned upside down, press firmly into the dough to create 3 circles. No Pyrex? No problem! Any 5" ish circle will do. Reform the leftovers from each sleeve and roll out to create the 4th round.

Place 2-3TB of the yummy filling in the center of each circle so that there is at least ¼" of edge still available once folded. Dip your finger in the water and run along the entire inside edge, then fold the circle and pat down. Use a fork to delicately mush-seal the edges and keep the delicious porky goodness safely inside. Place the folded, sealed empanadas on a cookie sheet and arrange them closely to maximize space. Brush the top of each one with the egg wash.

Bake for 10-12ish minutes at 400 degrees, checking after 8 minutes and swapping the baking sheet locations if necessary to even out the cooking. Bake until GBD (golden, brown and delicious).

165

Leslie Hart-Davidson

"If at first you don't succeed, try, try again." This proverb has been traced back to 'Teacher's Manual' by American educator Thomas H. Palmer, but the tasty sentiment also has roots in my husband BHD's culinary persistence. His willingness to try for over a year to create a beautiful, sweet, creamy, perfectly textured peanut butter pie that kicks the ass of restaurant imposter pies was, much like Lord Farquaad in Shrek, a sacrifice that I was willing to make to ensure the creation of a perfect dessert. Enjoy!

peanut butter pie

it's packed by weight, not volume.

Crust

1 pkg Lorna Doone cookies, crushed
1/2 stick butter, melted

Filling

1 C crunchy peanut butter
1 C less 2 TB confectioner's sugar (reserve the sugar)
2 TB honey
1 tsp vanilla extract
1 8 oz pkg cream cheese
1 Pint whipping cream
Peanuts for garnish

Yields: standard 9" pie
Pairs with: your redneck relatives and a chocolatini.
Consideration: this will ruin you for all other PB pies.

Directions

First things first: stick a medium sized metal bowl in the freezer.

For crust: Toss the cookies in a big baggie and smack the crap out of them until finely crushed. Melt the butter, then mix with the cookie dust and press firmly into a pie plate sprayed with cooking spray. Yes yes, I know this is a no-bake situation, but the damn crust will stick anyway if you don't spray it.

For filling: grab your mixer and go to town on the peanut butter, sugar, honey, vanilla extract, & cream cheese. Mix until fluffy and light, then set aside and clean the beaters.

(continued on next page)

Zero judgement from me if you lick them clean—just promise you'll unplug the mixer first.

Fetch the chilled metal bowl from the freezer and pour in the pint of whipping cream along with the 2 TB reserved sugar and scant 1/2 tsp of vanilla. Whippy dippy again with the mixer until super fluffy.

Grab a rubber spatula and plop 2/3 of the whipped cream into the center of the bowl containing the filling mixture. Gently fold the mixture from the outside over into the center until it juuuust comes together. Gently add more of the whippy dippy until you achieve a mousse-like texture.

Stick the pie in the fridge for up to 4 hours if possible, or quick freeze for an hour.

Options for serving all fancy-like: a garnish of peanuts, a dollop of whipped cream, and a chocolate drizzle on the plate.

whippy-dippy makes
the pie so good

good moms let kids lick the
beaters, but great moms
turn off the mixer first

169

Leslie Hart-Davidson

best in show

Baking is so very different from cooking. Baking is chemistry and science and all things measured in the world, but cooking...cooking is winging it and having fun and throwing shit in a pan with the luxury of knowing it'll alllll turn out just fine.

For the last decade, I've had a first-class ticket on the Baking Struggle Bus as I tried and failed to master the gooey contents of pie and finally, *finally* make my own crust. When I eventually got the goop content to set on a regular basis, I started to think about how I could level up my baking game. Since I'm just a wee bit competitive (those who know and love me are laughing hysterically at that), I set my sights on winning a blue ribbon from my county fair for pie.

In the summer of 2019, I entered my very first pretty pie in the Livingston County Fair in Michigan and crossed my fingers. The pie was a significant challenge since the baking day was 90+ degrees and not amenable to shaping into pretty flowers and lattices for the top crust. My working time was less than three minutes before popping the dough back into the freezer for another round. At several points in the process, I looked up and implored Fred, my late father-in-law and master baker, for his wisdom and guidance. I was pleased enough with the finished product to enter the Black and Blue Peach Pie. "Good luck!" the 4H lady said. "See you next week!"

It's tradition for my husband and kid and I to attend the fair each year to see the 4H animals, ride the rides, and eat the ridonkulous foods. The excitement of attending was magnified by a bazillion thanks to the pie entry, so I asked my family to indulge my curiosity and head straight to the 4H pavilion so we could check the results of judging. We walked through the corridor in search of the display and found the tiered presentation with dozens of net-covered pie slices and their accompanying ribbons. Our eyes scanned the entries once, twice, with no luck. There was no display of my pie. "I don't think I even placed," I told my family. I looked in the eyes of my teenage daughter and held back my tears. "It's ok," I explained. "It was my first try. I'll give it another shot next year. Let's go have some fun."

Food is Love

As we walked around the animal barns and had some indulgent food, my husband shook his head. "I want to go back and ask questions. I think it's odd that your pie wasn't even there. Besides, we need to get the carrying container." I reluctantly agreed, not wanting to be faced with my defeat again. He asked one of the concession workers in the pavilion where the containers would be. "Down thattaway," he said. Walking to the little table, I looked down and spotted my Tupperware. "WOOOOOOOOOOOOOOOOO!" I heard my husband yell, followed by my daughter's incredulous "OHMYGAWWWWWWD MOMMMM!" Startled by their shouts, I stepped back and saw what they were fussing about: the bulletin board directly above the container table with a photo of my pie and the Best in Show ribbon next to it.

I won't kid you here: I *instantly* started ugly crying. I was just so relieved that I didn't fail! I had zero expectations of the highest honor and honestly would have been tickled with just the blue ribbon. My daughter grabbed my face, wiped my tears and said "You did it! You rock! I'm so proud of you!" She looked at the folks strolling by and yelled "HEY! That's my mom! She won best in show!" My husband was just as thrilled, high-fiving the folks that walked past the ruckus we were causing. "Jump the gate and go hold up your pie!" he yelled. I entered the little display room where my pretty pie was waiting and picked up the slice. I was so charmed that the judges carefully sliced the piece to preserve the delicate flowers that I cried again, holding up my winning pie and the giant best in show ribbon and yelling "YAYYYY!" as my husband took the picture. I set the pie and my ribbon back down, looked up, and said "Thanks, Fred."

Black raspberries, blueberries, and peaches are the stars of this fruit pie recipe that earned me a Best in Show ribbon at the county fair. Black raspberries can be a challenge to find, so feel free to substitute red ones instead. I certainly won't judge if you choose to use a store-bought pie dough; it wasn't until recently that I finally learned how to make my own. Either way, food is love.

Dough
2 C flour
1 TB sugar
1 tsp salt
1 ½ sticks unsalted butter
½ stick butter flavored Crisco
4 TB ice water

Goop
2 C fresh black raspberries
1 C blueberries
1 C sliced yellow cling peaches
1 ½ C sugar
2 tsp cinnamon
1 tsp nutmeg
3 TB cornstarch

Yields: standard 9" pie
Pairs with: a strong competitive spirit.
Consideration: mixed berry pies are DA BOMB.

Dough
Cube the butter and shortening into cute little chunks, then place in a covered glass dish in the freezer. Sift together the dry ingredients and plop them in a food processor. Grab the chilled fat and pop in the food processor as well. Pulse several times until the fat chunks are incorporated and the mix looks like fat grains of sand that are just waiting to be molded into a cool shape.

Start adding a few TB of ice water and let the food processor whirl on low until the dough magically springs to life and becomes a giant clump. Remove and divide the dough into two even splats in cling wrap, then refrigerate while the goop is made and yell "THANK YOU" to the deceased relative in heaven who taught you that store bought dough is for suckers.

172
Food is Love

(continued on next page)

174

Food is Love

Goop

Rinse the blueberries and place in a saucepan with 1 C sugar, 1 tsp cinnamon and ½ tsp nutmeg over low/medium heat until sugary happiness is formed but before the blueberries break down (about 5 minutes). Set aside and allow to cool.

While the blueberries are blooping on the stove, place the rinsed blackberries and sliced peaches in a large bowl with ½ C sugar, 1 tsp cinnamon and ½ tsp nutmeg. Allow the mixture to macerate for 45 ish minutes, stirring occasionally and frequently snapping progress pics to text to friends who know you're super excited to be making Fair Pie. Combine the stove berries with the bowl berry mixture and gently stir. Add the cornstarch one TB at a time, folding together carefully to prevent berry breakage.

Preheat the oven to 350 degrees. Grab the refrigerated dough and roll out the first piece, placing gently in a 9" pie plate for the bottom crust. Add the goop mixture, allowing it to settle in place before conquering the top crust. No worries if you want a plain Jane top. The star of the show is the quality goop. Just be sure to add a few vent holes.

Bake at 350 degrees for an hourish, turning every 15 miutes until the crust is GBD (golden, brown and delicious).

Leslie Hart-Davidson

If you've ever driven the thruway in upstate New York, you know what a bitch it can be to travel in the winter. Remember the year that the Buffalo airport was buried under 7' of snow? About 3' fell in one day, which happened to be the day that my father-in-law Fred and brother-in-law Sean were driving from Ohio to Albany for a visit.

Luckily, they arrived safely about 15 hours later. I put a plate of beef stroganoff in front of Fred, who was still white-knuckled from the harried trip. He tucked in and didn't look up until his plate was spotless. The joy on his face when he finished and saw us staring at him was price-less. "That was GOOD," he said. The "Fred tuck-in" reaction is now the standard by which I judge all meals now.

beef stroganoff
screw Hamburger Helper – let's do this right.

2 lbs lean stew meat
½ C regular or GF flour
1 tsp each salt and pepper
½ stick butter
2 ½ C beef stock
2 TB Worcestershire
2 tsp Dijon mustard
1/3 C red wine
1 large yellow onion, diced
1 TB minced garlic
(or 3 cloves fresh)
8 oz can mushroom stems and
pieces (or 8 fresh fungus)
2/3 C sour cream
1 12 oz package wide egg noodles

Preheat oven to 400 degrees. In a dredge-worthy pan or plate, combine the flour, salt and pepper. Toss in each piece of stew meat, cutting in smaller uniform bite-sized chunks if desired. Flip the beef bits around until coated, then remove to a plate.

Heat the butter in a non-stick pan on medium heat. Plop in all the meaty bits and brown on the first side about 4 minutes, shaking the pan occasionally to prevent stick-ing. Flip the meaty bits to brown evenly on all sides, then give it a good stir.

(continued on the next page)

Serves: 4-6
Pairs with: a dramatic day.
Consideration: stroganoff can
be GF if you mind the beef
stock, flour and noodles.

Beef & noodles
fit for a Czar!

Add the beef stock, Worcestershire sauce and mustard. Stir a bit and bring it to a boil. Sploosh in the wine, then transfer the whole pan to a bigass oven-safe casserole dish with a lid.

Bake for 45 minutes, then pull out the rack (omg be careful), remove the lid and use a big spoon to scrape the sides and give it a good mix. Add the onions, garlic and fungus. Stir it up, minding the goo and not spilling it on the open oven door like a dumbass and making the kitchen stink.

Set a large pot of salted water on high heat about 10 minutes after the onions are added. When the water boils, cook the noodles according to package directions. Bake the stroganoff for another 20-30 minutes or however long you can stand it smelling so damn good. Once again, super carefully pull out the oven rack and remove the lid to bloop and blend in the sour cream, then stick it back in the oven another 10ish minutes until the sauce is warm.

Note: As a girl who orders sides of sour cream with the phrase "I'd like you to bring me enough sour cream that you're offended by the quantity," I have a note for the dairy doubters: it's okay if you skip the sour cream. The dish is tasty enough to serve without it. If there are picktastic eaters in your life who say "Ewwww cream sauces make me vomit," pull some of the goo out for them before you add the sour cream to the main dish. It's a win-win.

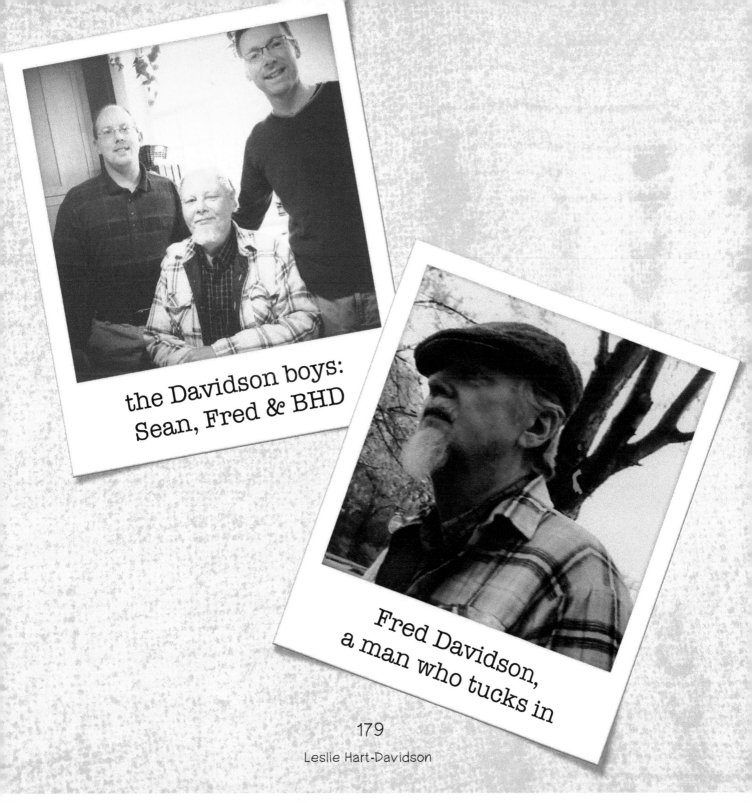

the Davidson boys:
Sean, Fred & BHD

Fred Davidson,
a man who tucks in

179

Leslie Hart-Davidson

500 Miles

From September 2017 until February of 2018, I traveled the 500 mile round trip each week from Michigan to Ohio to care for my brother in person three days at a time. I arranged all of his medical appointments and transported him to each one, conferenced weekly with the home health aides and his care coordinator, completed all the insurance and billing paperwork, and drove him the 80 mile round trip to each James Cancer Center visit.

When I wasn't physically in Ohio, I was in Michigan making calls and advocating for my brother. I'd check in with him daily, sending Star Wars memes and asking about the latest tv shows we were both watching. He was relentlessly positive and kind those first few months, never complaining once. In fact, his favorite nurse would frequently say "Greg, you wouldn't say shit if your mouth was full of it. I can't help you if you don't complain and tell me what hurts." He never did though, always focusing the conversation back to the other person. Greg would always ask about my husband and daughter, and press me for photos of my latest client projects.

At the same time I was taking care of Greg, I was also running my Interior Design business. My amazing HDD Studios team worked very hard to fill in the gaps while I was gone each week, taking on more of the project management and hands-on work so that I could do the very important job of taking care of my brother. While they were able to maintain the status quo, I wasn't able to pursue new business and grow our clientele, losing tens of thousands of dollars in potential business. I suspended my regular television appearances in Grand Rapids and put the writing of Food is Love on hold. Still, knowing the opportunity and concrete costs both up front and in hindsight, I chose to help my brother. If not for the amazing HDD Studios interns and staff, my seventeen-year-old business would have folded. There's not enough gratitude in the world for their service during those months.

BROTATO CHIP PART 3

My husband and 13 year old daughter were pretty good sports about my absence as well. Not many families could survive for that many months of chaos while a primary caregiver's attention was divided between states, but ours did. My daughter Lillian struggled with depression and her grades slipped while I was absent. I'd plan my trips to be back in time on the third day to fetch her from school. When she'd get in the car, I'd ask her about her week. "It's fine," she'd tell me. "Nothing you need to worry about. So how is Uncle Greg?" My teenage daughter protected me from her drama at school knowing that it would burden me too much to take on more. My husband and I fell into a weekly routine of logistics and coordination. With a hectic work schedule and intense academic job, his brain launched into survival mode. He constantly worried not only about my brother's health, but also my safety as I traveled so many miles in bad winter weather. My absence was challenging for him in many ways, but the 30+ years we had been together helped keep us strong.

Part of what kept me going during those months of care was the small victories and constant positive vibes from my brother. He had his eyes on the sci-fi prize of seeing Star Wars in December. On movie day, I walked Greg slowly to the car and took him to the theater. I helped him to his seat and made sure he was comfortable and had his new bucket list eyeglasses. I stole glances at him throughout the movie, making sure he was still awake and engaged. This was the first outing in four weeks other than a quick doctor visit, so I was concerned, but...he LOVED IT. We talked after the movie about the backstory and the cool effects and the general badassery of Rey. He thanked me about a thousand times for taking him, assuring me that this was one of the best days of his life.

> Greg assured me that this was one of the best days of his life.

Leslie Hart-Davidson

"I bet I could use Christmas lights in here," I told myself as I sprawled on the floor of my Holly Hobbie playhouse and stared at the vaulted cardboard ceiling. I grabbed the nearest doll and sought her opinion. "Whatcha think, Strawberry Shortcake?" I asked. I turned her head toward the ceiling, then back to meet my gaze. "I think Mom won't let you dig out the Christmas decorations in July. How about a lamp instead?" "Good point," I told my sweet-smelling friend, then hopped up to grab my Snoopy lamp and relocate it to my girl fort. The cord was too short to reach the outlet, so I headed to my brother's room to ask him for an extension cord.

It's the summer of 1979. I'm seven years old and in awe of my big brother. At age twelve (and a boy in the 70's), Greg can pretty much do anything he wanted: walk to a friend's house in the morning and not be back until the street lights are on, ride his bike as far as he wants through the neighborhood, set things on fire (mostly kidding there) and see scary movies. My parents had low expectations for his behavior: don't get arrested and don't make them have to call an ambulance. My jealousy of his age and freedom was intense, so when I asked Greg for an extension cord and he told me that he couldn't look for it because Mom was taking him to the movies, I instantly demanded to go as well.

"Umm, it's a scary movie. You'll hate it." he told me. "NO I WON'T!" I replied indignantly. "You don't even know what movie it is. Little girls can't go to this movie." That stung. "I'm GOING!" I told him, then convinced Mom to take me too. After assuring her that I didn't want to hang out at a friend's house instead, my Mom and brother reluctantly took me along.

The Regent theater in downtown Springfield smelled of popcorn and cigarettes. I stood at the candy counter and ordered a Pepsi and some Junior Mints, staring at all the movie posters and wondering which one I'm about to see big-girl style. "It's about a house," Greg told me during the drive. "Good. I like houses!" I replied as he offered a sly grin.

We found seats and I nestled deep in the red velvet, trying to plant my feet on the seat in front of me. I barely reached the back with my tiptoes. I was between my Mom and brother as the previews started, and I sat back to revel in my level of adulting. Amityville Horror began happily enough with sunshine and light and a lovely little family. About twenty minutes in, I realized that this movie isn't about a house; it's about a demonically possessed residence and HOLY SHIT THOSE FLIES! THOSE FLIES ARE ALL OVER THE PRIEST! OMG! My mouth gaped open and a Junior Mint dropped out. My brother snickered as I hopped up. I plopped my Pepsi in Mom's lap and told her I had to pee. I ran out of the theater and made it just in time to puke up soda and chocolate in the vintage sink of the Regent bathroom. Luckily, I was alone in the bathroom and had a minute to collect myself. That was the scariest scene I've ever watched in a movie. The Blob, which previously held the number one spot in my scary list, wasn't even a close second anymore. What had I been thinking when I demanded to come along? "Ohhhh," I thought. "I wanted to be big. I wanted to be brave like Greg."

I tidied up my terrycloth tank top, rinsed the sink, and wiped my mouth. I decided to channel my inner Greg and go sit bravely to watch the rest of the movie. "Just pretend you're safe in your Holly Hob-

bie house," I told myself. I returned to my seat and thanked Mom for holding my drink. She eyed me to make sure I could continue. I nodded. Greg looked over at me. "You good?" he asked. "All good," I said, then turned my attention back to the gore. I snuck looks at him during the movie, checking for cues of his facial expression on how to enjoy the movie. I learned from him. I learned how to be brave.

Greg was admitted to the hospital yesterday with complications from his chemo treatment. Since September my brother has been watching my face for cues of how to be brave during this insane shit show of cancer treatment, not realizing that I'm only brave because of him. I'm still occasionally puking up metaphorical Junior Mints in the bathroom, but each time I tidy myself up and go back to my seat next to Greg, ready to watch until the end.

putter-offers

In my second book **It's Not Your Room, it's You**, I examined five types of home improvement Putter-Offers who failed to take action with their spaces even in the face of significant need. Having spent decades feeding people and talking with them about their relationships with food, I've identified 7 types of meal Putter-Offers who choose not to make cooking a priority for themselves or their families. Let's take a look at the hallmarks of each Putter-Offer and how to overcome the no-meal mindset by removing the obstacles for cooking.

"Take Out Binder" Kitchen

Years ago when working with design clients to remodel their kitchen, I realized how differently people use their kitchens. "We want the best of everything!" was the direction given by the Flashy McFlashington couple about their kitchen remodel. "A Wolf 6 burner stove, granite countertops, custom cabinetry—everything in this magazine picture. THIS picture" Mrs. McFlashington pointed menacingly with her perfectly manicured index finger. "Certainly, but could you first please tell me about who cooks and how you'll use the kitchen on a daily basis?" The McFlashingtons looked at each other, then back at me. "Just give us this picture." the wife said. "But add one thing: a bookcase here where I can store the binder with all the takeout menus." Mr. McFlashington nodded, then stated "We don't cook. We're just doing this for resale."

I looked carefully at the couple. "Soooo your budget is nearly six figures for a shelf that holds your takeout menus?" "Right!" they said.

Leslie Hart-Davidson

putter-offers scaredy-cooks

Lacking a knowledge base for all things kitchen is unfortunately becoming a more common reason that folks don't want to tackle cooking. If you didn't have parents who prepared meals often (my mama preferred a boiled hot dog with white rice for most dinners) or weren't exposed to dinners at Grandma's house, then the closest thing to cooking education you could claim would be 7th grade Home Ec or watching The Food Network. Not cool.

I promise you that cooking isn't scary. As my hero Alton Brown describes it, "Heat + Food = Cooking." Let's try these baby steps to get you in the kitchen:

1. **Watch a shit-ton of Tasty.co videos**
    These 2 minutes informative and delicious beauties pop up in social media feeds constantly and are a great source of well-produced and easy to follow recipes. Their website's catalog of "easy" and "low stress" meals are perfect for the beginner and can empower you to try out a few easy dishes.

2. **Spend time with cooktastic friends**
    If you have pals that cook with some level of skill, offer to buy the groceries for a meal and ask them to narrate what they're doing and give you prep tasks to demystify the process. Hell, while you're at it, offer up adult beverages to go along with the meal to ease the pain of constantly asking questions, like "what does BROWN mean? How do I know when the sauce is THICK?" Just think of all the Insta-worthy stories you can create on your food journey!

3. Invest in a few cookware pieces

Michelangelo didn't use shitty paint brushes, and Tony Hawk didn't ride a skateboard that he picked up at Five Below. A decent 12" non-stick skillet (rounded sides) and the same size sauté pan (straight sides) with a lid will be a great start to your collection. Add a cutting board and a decent chef's knife, and you're ready to roll! For more specific deets on what you need to be successful in the kitchen, check out Alton Brown's *Gear for Your Kitchen*.

4. Just fucking try

Seriously, just practice cooking. You don't get good at a musical instrument or playing a sport without practice, so put in your time in the kitchen. Good cooks aren't born; they're baked though a long process of learning. There's zero shame in burning something or ruining a sauce if it's in the process of trying. Each attempt gets you closer to a better meal, so just do a post-mortem on any failed meal failed attempts and find what went wrong in order to level up. You've got this.

Leslie Hart-Davidson

stromboli basics

Nearly every culture has a variation of dough plus filling. The stromboli is a braided dough with many variations of delicious innards. Here are the standard instructions for four of my favorite stromboli recipes.

Lay out the dough: Preheat oven to 375 degrees. Be brave and open the scary loud-popping tube of thin pizza dough (or hand it to your kid to open, hiding your face in shame—whatevs), spreading it open into a large, even rectangle on either parchment or non-stick foil-lined baking sheet. Splash on about 1 TB of the evoo and use the back of a spoon to spread it evenly over the entire top of the dough. This is the perfect time to jazz up the dough with spices that complement the rest of the ingredients!

Fill the center: Divide the dough mentally into thirds lengthwise. All the interior ingredients will go along the center third, so use your best Barbara Billingsly *Airplane!* quotes while sprinkling shit along the "runway." Yes, your ingredients will speak jive.

Braidy Bit: It's go time for the braid. First, take a sharp knife and cut matching tentacles about 1" wide down each long side of the rectangle. You'll end up with about 12 cuts (13 tentacles) on each side. Start at the top right and pull the tentacle across to meet the beginning of the opposite tentacle. Bring the left tentacle across to meet the right, then repeat the process back and forth until you've reached the bottom. On the last ten-

Food is Love

tacle, create a butt and tuck the end under the opposite side, squishing the bottom seam together to prevent the innards from spilling out the bum.

When the tentacles are in place and you have an awesome little mummy wrap, add the drizzle of choice and do the back-of-spoon thing again to spread it evenly.

Bake and Top: Place the Stromboli in the oven and bake for about 6 minutes, then turn the pan so it finishes evenly for another 5 or so minutes. When the crust is beautifully golden

brown, remove from oven and place on a cooling rack for 5ish minutes. Move to a cutting board and slice into breadstick-width chunks for serving.

191

My dear friend & book manager Sara's stepson Bobber learned how to make Stromboli to earn a Boy Scout badge at age 9. Luckily, he shared the recipe and technique with me one evening as Sara and I were working on my first book. "He's making us dinner?" I asked her. "Like ya do," she replied. I watched carefully as junior chef Bobber kicked ass in the kitchen and realized that anyone can rock a Stromboli.

Bobber's Stromboli
is that the one with the mummy wrap?

1 tube thin crust
Pillsbury pizza dough
1 C pepperoni
2 C mozzarella cheese, divided
2 TB parmesan cheese
2 TB evoo, divided
1 TB, plus 1 tsp Italian
seasoning (the grindy kind)
Marinara sauce for dipping

Serves: 4
Pairs with: a hoppy craft beer, like M-43 from Old Nation.
Consideration: if a 9 year-old can make this, you can too.

After you've laid out the dough (see page 190), grind about 1 TB of the Italian seasoning over the evoo.

Sprinkle half of the mozzarella cheese down the center third runway, then check your Vector, Victor for the pepperoni. Arrange them in a pretty layer so they're juuuuust slightly overlapping, but not too overcrowded. Top the pepperoni with the remaining mozzarella and clutch your pearls. See braidy bit instructions on page 190.

Grind on 1 tsp more Italian seasoning, then sprinkle the parmesan cheese over the top. Bake and finish like page 191 instructs you. Serve with marina sauce for dipping.

Having learned the 'boli basics from a 9 year-old kid, I took a leap beyond the traditional pepperoni and thought about how I could level up the filling. Alternative pork and some greens sounded like a good start, so spinach and prosciutto Stromboli was born.

1 tube thin crust
Pillsbury pizza dough
2 C fresh spinach, wilted
1 5 oz package prosciutto
2 C mozzarella cheese, divided
2 TB parmesan cheese
2 TB evoo, divided
1 TB plus 1 tsp Italian
seasoning (the grindy kind)
Marinara sauce for dipping

Directions

After you've laid out the dough (see page 190), grind 1 tsp of Italian seasoning over the evoo. Fill a shallow pan with ½ inch of water and get it simmering over medium heat. Drop the spinach in and DO NOT WALK AWAY. Move it around with tongs until it starts to soften and wilt, about 45 seconds. Remove the wilted bits to a paper towel-lined plate to dry off a minute.

Sprinkle half of the mozzarella cheese down the center of the runway. Peel off a strip of prosciutto and bunch it up a bit, evenly placing the porky pillows along the center. Top the prosciutto with the wilted spinach, then cover with the remaining mozzarella. Wrap it up, mummy style (see page 190), grind on 1 tsp more Italian seasoning, then sprinkle the parmesan cheese over the top. Bake and finish like page 191 instructs.

any shaved deli meat would be a welcome substitute or addition

Serves: 4
Pairs with: a third date with someone you are trying to impress.
Consideration: Tasty leftovers.

Being a giant fan of craft breweries, I'm always tickled when I can have a beer *and* delicious food. New Holland Brewery in Grand Rapids, MI had a flatbread pizza on their menu years ago that featured thin pear slices, walnut chunks and a honey swirl. I upcycled the idea into a Stromboli, using the honey as a final drizzle on the braid. It's stupid good (especially with a Hoptronix beer).

pear & walnut stromboli
man buns optional for baking.

1 tube thin crust Pillsbury pizza dough
1 Anjou or other sweet pear, sliced thin and seeds removed
½ C arugula
⅓ C diced walnuts
½ C shredded parmesan cheese, divided
⅛ C gorgonzola cheese
Ground black pepper
2 TB evoo, divided
1 TB honey

Serves: 4
Pairs with: a spoiled pomeranian.
Consideration: excellent bougie brunch fare.

Lay out the magic dough (see page 190), then grind some fresh black pepper over the evoo.

Sprinkle half of the parmesean cheese down the runway. Arrange the thinly, sliced pears in a pretty layer so they're juuuust slightly overlapping, but not too overcrowded. Toss the walnuts over the pears. Arugula is next, followed by dots of the gorgonzola. Rock the braidy bit (See page 190).

Sprinkle the other half of the parmesan cheese over the top, then do a pretty swishy thing with the honey. Hit it one more time with black pepper. Follow the baking instructions on page 191 and dig in!

no arugula?
spinach or
basil work
great!

197

When my teenage niece Rae would visit during school vacations, I would give her cooking lessons. Stromboli in all forms is a fun meal, so I taught her the dessert version to try out at home. Forgetting the proper term for the meal, she later texted this: "Aunt Leslie, what's the strombooty thing again?" Yup, that'll do.

nutella strombooty
is there really such a thing as too much Nutella, mama?

1 tube thin crust Pillsbury pizza dough
4 TB nutella
¾ C whipped cream cheese (an 8 oz container is about 1 cup)
1 TB cinnamon, divided

Serves: 4
Pairs with: a break up.
Consideration: though tempting, slathering on too much cream cheese makes for squishy 'boli.

Prep the dough for basic 'boli as outlined on page 190. Sprinkle cinnamon in a light layer evenly over the entire top of the dough.

Dot the 4 tablespoons of Nutella evenly down the center runway like gingerman buttons, then check your Vector, Victor and spread the chocolatey goo with a spatula down the center.
Next, splat ¾ of a tub of whipped cream cheese in the middle and spread it evenly down the runway. Sprinkle the remaining cinnamon over the top. Braid it up (see page 190), then bake and finish (see page 191).

Serve with the strawberry goo, found on page 200 and some aerosol whipped cream.

you can totally
top with choco-
late syrup, too

Channel your inner Liz Lemon: you want to go to there. The goal is to make a gloopy bloop that makes sweet happiness over a thingy like dessert or pancakes or your mouth. There are many ways to get there. You do you, boo.

strawberry goo
wait - it's that easy?

1 cup finely diced ripe
strawberries
2 tsp sugar

Dice the berries and place in a bowl. Sprinkle sugar over the top and mix well. Leave the berries to macerate for an hourish while the Nutella strombooty cooks. Place in a baggie, lay flat on the counter, then mash the crap out of the berries with a mallet or a can from your pantry or *Pulp Fiction* character Jules' wallet. Feel free to go at it with an immersion blender if you have one handy. Use a spoon to drip the happiness over the target.

Yields: 1 cup, just enough for a dessert stromboli.
Pairs with: a break up or anything that needs a sweet kick in the pants.

goo keeps great
in a squirt bot-
tle in the fridge
for days

table for one

Okay, I get it. You live alone and don't like to make a big mess over a meal just for yourself. It's hard to cook in a single serving size, so the idea of eating the same meal for lunch and dinner three days in a row gives you indigestion. It also might seem like a big production to make a full meal when you're just going to sit in front of the tv and binge watch a whole show season on Netflix anyway. Here are some tactics to help you find some happiness in the kitchen solo:

1. **Make friends with the butcher**
   When you see something in the case that looks delicious but is too large, ask the butcher nicely to cut it down. I've never had a butcher say no to a special request, so just ask what's possible while you're perusing the meats. If you catch a good sale on a larger cut (like pork or beef tenderloins,) the butcher can even wrap or vacuum seal individual portions for freezing.

2. **Remember that you deserve to eat well**
   You want a full meal with all the trimmings? Eat the damn full meal with allllll the trimmings. Go whole hog and enjoy the shit out of your kitchen time. Grab a tasty beverage, crank some tunage and cook. Be happy in your kitchen! There's no reason why you can't eat well every day. Your relationship status has zero bearing on your ability to dine well, so take advantage of your total menu control and eat whatever you want, whenever you want.

3. **Portion and freeze**

In the event that you do end up with tons of leftovers after cooking, invest in some decent freezer storage bags or containers and label them well. If you've had a long day, it's lovely to go shopping in your own freezer and have a crazy tasty dinner 20ish minutes later.

4. **Pay it forward**

If you're just not a fan of leftovers or freezer meals, that's totally ok. I understand the culinary repeat reluctance, so think about this before you toss any extras: who else would enjoy this meal? Do you have an elderly neighbor who might appreciate something home-cooked? Do you have family nearby that would enjoy a tasty treat? How about a coworker who usually eats sad, lonely frozen meals for lunch? If you can think of anyone who would benefit from the happiness of homecookery, get it in their hands. Food is love, ya know.

Leslie Hart-Davidson

Hellsyeah naan pizza! The small version of this yummo Indian bread is an absolutely perfect substrate for personalized pizzas when you have a picky family or crowd. Naanzzas also work great for parties when you make multiple varieties and cut them into halves or for sharing.

1 mini naan
1 ½ TB tomato sauce or pesto
⅓ C shredded parmesan cheese
¼ C artichoke hearts
1 slice prosciutto, ripped into bits

1. Add 1 ½ TB sauce and swoosh around to the edges
2. Sprinkle on ¼-⅓ C cheese
3. Add ¼ C chopped veggies
4. Plop on ¼ C meats or nuts (if you're rocking a vegetarian version, double the veg quotient)
5. Finish with any seasonings or herbs to taste

Baking
Preheat the oven (regular or toaster) to broil. On a baking sheet, place the naked naan on nonstick foil or parchment and prepare the ingredients. Build your naanzza according to the guidelines and broil on low for 5ish minutes, turning halfway through to brown evenly. The goal is to melt the cheese and warm the whole kit & kaboodle with a slight browning of the toppings. Cut into share-size shapes if desired and serve immediately!

Directions
No matter what toppings you add, follow these 5 simple steps for a delicious naanzza.

Yields: one personal 'zza
Pairs with: indecision.
Consideration: build and bake up to 4 at a time on one sheet.

naanzza
it's a "choose your own adventure" meal.

Food is Love

Baby naans are sold in a package of 4 and are about 7oz total weight, resembling the size of your hand

205

Naanza Topping Ideas

Sauce
Tomato/Marinara
Bechamel
Alfredo
Pesto
Hummus
Barbeque
Pumpkin Puree
Applesauce
Sour Cream
Infused EVOO

Cheese
Mozzarella
Provolone
Parmesan
Gouda
Bleu
Romano
Ricotta
Cheddar
Goat

Veg*
Onion
Shallots
Tomatoes (fresh or sundried)
Peppers (bell or banana)
Spinach
Kale
Carrots
Mushrooms
Garlic
Olives
Artichoke Hearts
Capers

Protein
Pepperoni
Bacon
Sausage
Pork (ham, prosciutto)
Chicken (shredded, chunked)
Beef (shredded or ground)
Anchovies
Salmon
Tofu
Nuts (walnuts,
pine nuts, cashews)

Seasonings
Salt and pepper
Italian Blend Flakes
Red Pepper Flakes
Cumin
Oregano
Cinnamon
Tabasco
Frank's Red Hot Sauce
Honey

Herbs
Cilantro
Oregano
Mint
Basil
Thyme
Dill
Parsley
Sage

* whether wilted, steamed, sautéed or roasted, you do you boo

Food is Love

Wacky
- Pumpkin puree
- Mozz & gouda
- Crispy kale
- Roasted red pepper
- Sautéed onion
- Bacon
- Cinnamon

Traditional
- Pesto
- Parm cheese
- Artichoke hearts
- Prosciutto
- Red pepper flakes

Savory
- BBQ
- Blue cheese
- Carrot slivers
- Shredded chicken
- Tabasco drizzle

fancy pork
- Bacon
- Spinach
- Mozzarella

mediterranean
- Sundried Tomato
- Spinach
- Tomato
- Feta

classic
- Pepperoni
- Mozzarella
- Tomato Sauce

LHD's fav
- Brussel Sprouts
- Bacon
- Parmesean

Leslie Hart-Davidson

Do you recall the Gordon Elliott tv show from the 90's called *Door Knock Dinners*? Gordon would walk through a suburban neighborhood, pound on a random door and invite himself and a famous chef inside to raid the unsuspecting homeowner's pantry. The chef would prepare an amazing meal using only what was on hand while Gordon distracted the family. I have a vague recollection of one chef proudly declaring "I found a jar of maraschino cherries, two soy sauce packets and a freezer-burned package of chicken breasts. Brilliant!" Now, I know you'd never let your food situation get that dire, riiiight? Right. It's challenging to stare into the abyss of your pantry or the shelves of your refrigerator and have zero insight for a meal. Even if you do have plenty of ingredients, it's still so, soooo easy to just summon food from your phone if you don't have a clue what to make for dinner. Before you resort to take-out again, look at these awesome ways to find dinner inspiration:

1. **Think seasonally**
   Trust me when I tell you that sometimes it's okay to go to the store without a plan for dinner. If you shop hungry and without a list, you might spend an extra $20 on impulse goodies, but you might also see some fresh ingredients or a crazy awesome sale that inspires your meal that evening. One of my best last-minute meals was courtesy of a massive display of sweet corn on the cob (Midwest girl right here), the most beautiful heirloom tomato I've ever seen, and a mouthwatering display of fresh chicken and spinach bratwurst from the butcher's case. Sold! It takes a flexible mindset and a bit of cooking skill to make up meals on the fly, but the payoff can be incredible.

2. Make a list

Ok guys, I'm totally serious right now: I have a master list called the "Oink Bok Splash Moo" guide with meals that I prepare in heavy rotation categorized by pork, poultry, seafood and beef recipes. Whenever I think "Hmmm...I don't know what I should make for dinner," I pull out the list from the front of my recipe binder and look for inspiration. It's super handy to have every meal possibility right in front of me like my own personal menu. You can edit your master menu seasonally as well to reflect ingredient availability and outdoor temps (beef stroganoff on a 110 degree day is NOT A THING.)

3. Start with NO

I'm stealing this idea from my world of interior design when I first work with clients and ask them what they DON'T want their new space to look like. "No Mid-Century Modern," some will say. "I hate Arts and Crafts," say others. "If you give me green walls, I'll vomit" was a real client quote. Along those lines, think about what food categories *don't* sound appetizing at that moment. Maybe your uterus is telling you that dainty salads are OUT, or perhaps anything too spicy will keep you up all night. Just had Italian for lunch? No pasta for dinner. Rule out the undesirable menu options and go from there.

4. Just fucking Google it

Wrap your hungry brain around this number: fifty-nine million. That's the number of search results Google returned when I entered "What's for dinner" in the search bar. Between Google, Pinterest, and so many cooking-related websites, you have zero excuses for not finding something yummy for dinner. In fact, if you have a specific ingredient and want to find out what you could make with it, Googling recipes with that item can narrow your search considerably.

209

P

asta with whatevs is a true "choose your own adventure" meal that can be created from pantry goodies or bits & pieces lurking in the refrigerator. As long as you follow these general guidelines, you can learn to wing it with any ingredients for this fast, fun pasta dish. Here's the recipe for the shrimp and asparagus pasta shown. Check out the chart on page 212 to create your own!

¾ lb spaghetti
⅛ C regular evoo, divided
1 bunch asparagus, chopped
1 lb thawed raw shrimp
3 TB butter
1 lemon, cut in wedges
¼ C freshly grated parmesan cheese
3 TB Italian herb evoo
Salt and pepper to taste

Directions

In a large pot, bring 4 quarts of salted water to a boil. Cook pasta according to package directions. Drain, but reserve a cup of the cooked pasta water when finished.

While the pasta is cooking, grab a nonstick pan. Heat 2 TB evoo on medium high heat and toss in the asparagus. Generously salt and stir the chopped stalks while you think about how your pee will smell funny later, about 5 minutes. The asparagus should be fork tender and bright in color.

Reduce the heat to medium and add the butter pats. Plop in the raw shrimp and stir to coat. Continue moving and turning the sea critters until they become pinkish and curled like the letter C, about 3 minutes. Add tong-fulls of the cooked pasta, stirring between additions. Supplement with regular evoo and reserved pasta water until the noodles are all coated evenly. Sprinkle parmesan cheese over the top and give it another swish.

Remove from heat. Add lemon juice from half the wedges along with the Italian herb evoo and give it one last mix. Serve with fresh ground black pepper.

remember: flavored evoo is always added OFF the heat at the very end

Serves: 4
Pairs with: a bottle of wine to get your creative juices flowing. Don't be afraid to experiment!

Pasta with Whatevs

Pasta
Spaghetti
Linguini
Rotini
Shells
Penne
Elbows
Buccatini

Sautéed Veggies
Onion
Mushrooms
Cherry Tomatoes
Bell Pepper (any color)
Zuchinni
Yellow Squash
Asparagus
Baby Corn

Seasoning
Lawry's Seasoning
Cumin
Pepper
Garlic
Lemon Juice
Sea Salt
Chili Powder
Black Pepper

Protein
Tofu
Chicken
Steak
Seafood (shrimp, scallops, mussels)
Bacon
Ground Beef

Wilted Stuff
Spinach
Arugula
Basil

Cheese
Parm
Romano
Mozzarella
Goat

Sauce
Marinara
Alfredo
EVOO & Butter
Flavored Oil
Pesto

212

Food is Love

Red & Green
Penne
Steak Slices
Red Bell Pepper
Pesto
Shaved Parmesean

Gluten Free Spirals
Lobster
Sundried Tomatoes
Broccolini
Shaved Parmesean
Butter & evoo

Bow Tie Pasta
Bacon
Chopped Tomato
Fresh Basil
Butter & evoo

Earthy Goodness
Linguini
Mushrooms
Garlic
Arugula
Alfredo

Fusilli Pasta
Cherry Tomato
Wilted Spinach
Shredded Parmesean
Butter & evoo

Veggie Delight
Shells
Zucchini
Yellow Squash
Onion
Marinara

Leslie Hart-Davidson

Dayyyyyyam we're busy. Schlepping and shuttling and running about, always on the go, fetching kids and dropping off kids and working your buns off. Cooking can seem like just another pain-in-the-ass chore after a long day of the office grind and taxi service for the little ones, but I assure you that a decent meal after a long day can be a salvation rather than just another item on the to-do list. Here are some ways to making cooking a reality when you're short on the precious commodity of time:

1. **Plan ahead**
   Yes, yes, I know it sucks to sit down and think about what you're going to eat for the week, but there's nothing worse than the moment your stomach is rumbling and you're rushing to ferry kids from one event to another and realize that you don't have any meal-worthy groceries at home. "Pizza it is," you think regretfully for the fifth time that month. In the time it takes you to nuke a sad little frozen dinner, you can plan out meals for the week based on which days are crazier than the others. Since you need to stir the sad little frozen meal and pop it back in for another couple minutes, you now have time to make a grocery list for all the items you need to complete those easy meals.

2. **Crock it!**
   I can throw a meatsicle in the crock pot with some bags of veg and a liquid in the morning faster than I can brush my teeth. What's a meatsicle, you ask? Whatever meat package is closest to my hand when I reach in the freezer. Sometimes it's a 2-3lb pack of chicken thighs, sometimes it's country style pork ribs. In my busiest weeks, whatever I have on hand is

what's crocked that day. Imagine the joy of walking in the house after a long day of work and smelling your yummy dinner awaiting you. Crock pots are a total, delightful, time-saving THING!

3. **Be a Weekend Warrior**
   If your weeknights aren't conducive to cooking because of over-scheduling or grueling commutes, consider taking a few hours on a Saturday or Sunday to get a jump start on cooking for the week ahead. Being mindful about your meal planning will allow you hit the grocery and get all the items you need to whip up a few things that can be crocked or baked with ease. Pinterest has thousands of pins for make-ahead meals (fair warning: falling down the rabbit hole of Pinterest food boards can take more time than making the actual meals.) The weekend food projects can be individually portioned and frozen with instructions right on the package so you can spend more time with your kids figuring out "new math" homework and less time chopping broccoli (cue Dana Carvey).

I'll probably take some shit for this recipe from Parm Purists because there's no breading on the chicken. I gave up that part of the recipe years ago to save both time and carbs, so the current incarnation is really more of a "Chicken Cheese" thing. Scoff all you want, but this dish is wicked fast and wicked good.

1 lb chicken breast tenders
1 24 oz jar pasta sauce
4 C shredded Italian cheese
2 tsp minced garlic
1/2 lb pasta
Salt & pepper

Directions

Preheat the oven to broil. Pour the majority of the sauce in a pan and set it on simmer to heat. Add a sploosh of tap water (about ¼ C) to the jar with the remaining sauce and replace the lid. Shakey shakey, then pour the watered-down mixture in the bottom of a 9 x 13 Pyrex pan. Tilt the pan back and forth to cover the bottom evenly.

Lay out a sheet of waxed paper about 2' long on a flat counter. Place the chicken tenders close together, then cover with another piece of waxed paper. Pound the tenders to a uniform thickness of a smartphone using a paillard mallet (thanks, Martha Stewart) or a rolling pin. Sprinkle on salt and pepper.

Heat a nonstick pan with the evoo and sauté the tenders over medium heat until the first side is cooked. It'll be white and have a bit of pretty browning on it. Flip the tenders to repeat on the raw side, adding the minced garlic to the pan. Use tongs to spread the garlic around evenly. When the second side is cooked through, remove all of the pieces to the Pyrex pan and lay them in rows,.

Sprinkle on the shredded cheese evenly. Place in the oven to melt and broil the cheese. Watch carefully to prevent burning and pull the Pyrex pan when the top is your favorite shade of brown.

chicken parm
tits. we are having tits for dinner.

Food is Love

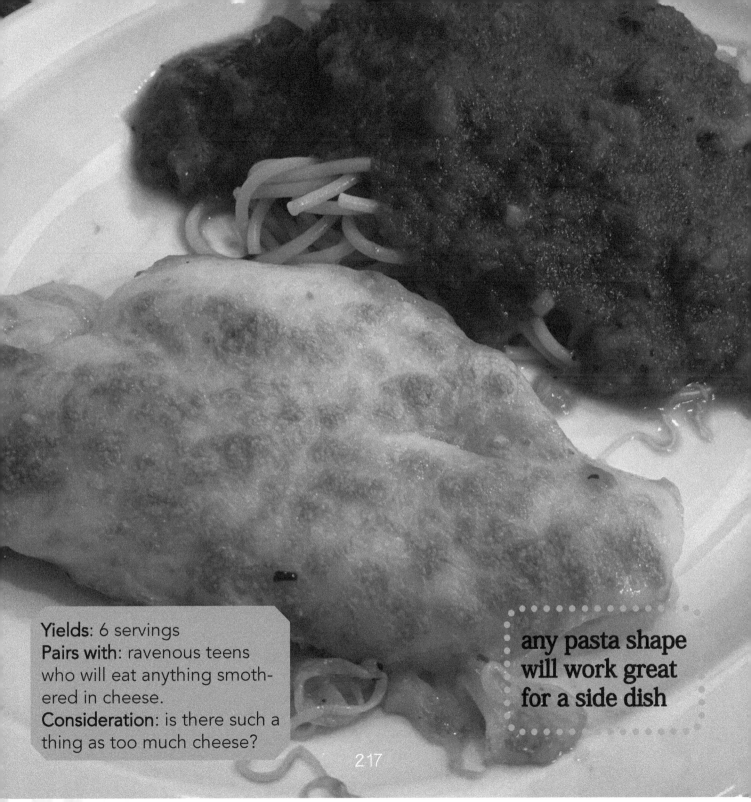

Yields: 6 servings
Pairs with: ravenous teens who will eat anything smothered in cheese.
Consideration: is there such a thing as too much cheese?

any pasta shape will work great for a side dish

My sister-in-law Amy comes to visit for girl time frequently and loves to send me recipe inspiration for our meals. Her husband is a picky mofo, but her culinary palette is far more adventurous. This dish has evolved into an easy weeknight almost-one-pot version that's incredibly delicious and quick. Thanks, Amy!

quickie carbonara
heart happy, but not heart healthy.

1 rotisserie chicken (or chunks of prepackaged chicken, about 1 ½ cups)
3 TB evoo
6 slices thick cut bacon, chopped
6 slices deli style Mozzarella or provolone cheese
1 ½ C heavy cream
½ tsp black pepper
Salt to taste
¾ C chicken broth
1 TB chopped garlic
¾ C freshly grated Parmesan cheese
1 ½ C fresh spinach, chopped
1 C sun dried tomatoes, chopped
1 box of linguine or other favorite pasta shape

Preheat the oven to 450 degrees.

Chop up the rotisserie chicken into bite-sized bits, then set aside. You can use any kind of leftover chicken or the prepackaged chunks from the deli.

In a large oven-safe pan, add the chopped bacon bits under medium high heat and cook until crumbly and happy. Remove the porktastic goodness to a paper towel, then scoop out all but a few tablespoons of bacon grease.

Put on water to boil for pasta and follow package directions.

 (continued on the next page)

Yields: 6 servings
Pairs with: wine and gossip.
Consideration: ribbons of sundried tomatoes are the best texture.

rice is a fine substitute for pasta

While the water begins to boil boil toil and trouble, reduce the bacon pan heat to medium and toss in the garlic. Swish around for about a minute, then add in the heavy cream, chicken broth, salt, pepper and parmesan cheese.

Swishy swishy until the cheese melts, but don't let the heavy cream boil.

Add in your spinach and sun-dried tomatoes and allow it to simmer until the spinach starts to wilt, about one minute.

Evenly plop the chicken chunks around the pan. Sprinkle the bacon bits over top, then lovingly cover the whole damn pan with deli cheese slices. Place the pan in the oven under the broiler to melt for a hot minute until it turns your version of golden brown. Serve over pasta or rice portions and enjoy the carb coma.

Food is Love

Derps, Dogs, Etc.

221

Leslie Hart-Davidson

ramificooking

Unfortunate ramifications of cooking including messy counters and many dirty dishes.

Allow me to get my geek on for a moment to quote Uncle Ben Parker: "With great power comes great responsibility." When you use your time and energy to cook, what always comes along for the ride is a dirty mess. I get it--you hate doing dishes with the passion of ten thousand burning suns. Multi-step meals make you cringe with the thought of having pots and pans and measuring cups and utensils all mocking you from the sink awaiting a good scrub. I still have flashbacks from college days when the dishes would pile up like the Leaning Tower of Pisa until a roommate broke down from the sadness of eating goulash from a coffee mug and finally washed the damn dishes.

I understand how crappy it can be when a dishwasher is missing from your appliance suite, so here are a few ways to help Ramificooking Putter-Offers combat their fear of accumulating and washing dishes:

1. **Clean as you go**
   Here's an analogy for you: think about how putting all of your loose coins or single dollar bills in a jar at night adds up substantially after a few months. You probably don't miss that money, right? Sneaky little actions taken a fraction at a time make it easier than waiting until the end of the month and transferring $100 to your savings account. I want you to think about dishes the same way: treat each measuring cup or mixing

bowl like loose change and just get it done while you have it in front of you. Since cooking generally involves down time between steps while things are simmering or baking, you can knock out a few dishes and wipe down counters while you're waiting.

2. Up your infrastructure game

If your dish rack and kitchen scrubbie came from the Dollar Store, it's no wonder you hate doing dishes. Investing in a decent drying rack that features slots for cutlery and a flexible area for both plates and pans is a total game-changer: suddenly there's a smart space to put clean items as you work through the process. Your choice of scrubbie can make a huge difference too. Test out different styles: the wand with dish soap in the handle and scrubbie on the head, basic rectangle with sponge on one side and brillo-ish material on the other, a rag, or a steel wool disc. All of these have pros and cons, so try each to determine what works most effectively for you (and be sure to follow manufacturer's recommendations on delicate bits—your Teflon will never make it through an encounter with a steel wool pad.)

3. Rock one-pot meal recipes

An awesome game plan for minimal dishes is just opening a bunch of cans and throwing shit into a single pot. It's healthier than a frozen meal (and way less sad) and usually doesn't take a ton of time. If you prefer fresh veg over canned, check out the produce convenience area at your local grocery store. They often have pre-cut packages of veggies for things like stir fry. A one-step oven meal can use those veggies as well—layering a Pyrex casserole dish with veg and seasoned chicken breasts can yield a tasty and easy clean-up meal. Think of your dinner as an exercise in assembly rather than cooking and you'll minimize the ramificooking effects.

223

4. Embrace the Disposables

Target's aisle of food storage options is a glorious place. The rows of plastic containers and baggies are as diverse as a Benneton ad, but that's not the coolest part: the food prep items are the stars of this aisle. Reynolds created a line of crazy convenient disposable plastic baking bags for ovens and slow cookers that cut out all need for washing dishes. They also manufacture foil pans for casseroles and lasagnas that can be tossed after baking. The Earth will cry a little bit, but hey, at least you're conserving water. If you want to go one disposable step further, toss some paper plates in your cart at Target. While a little bit of my soul will die every time you use a paper plate instead of a pretty dinner plate, I'll be comforted with the idea that you're eating real food instead of hitting up a Taco Bell drive thru.

Ramificooking can be beneficial too! Take the remaining stock from the Crocked Whole Chicken on Page 226 after you remove clucky and strain the liquid gold through a colander into a large bowl. Cover and place in the fridge for a few hours or until the next day. Scrape off the top layer of fat and use the gelatinous bits to infuse with your crack mashed taties (page 56) or Stubborn Kid Pasta (page 232). You can even make chicken and noodles with the leftover clucky bits. This technique works for any crocked meat.

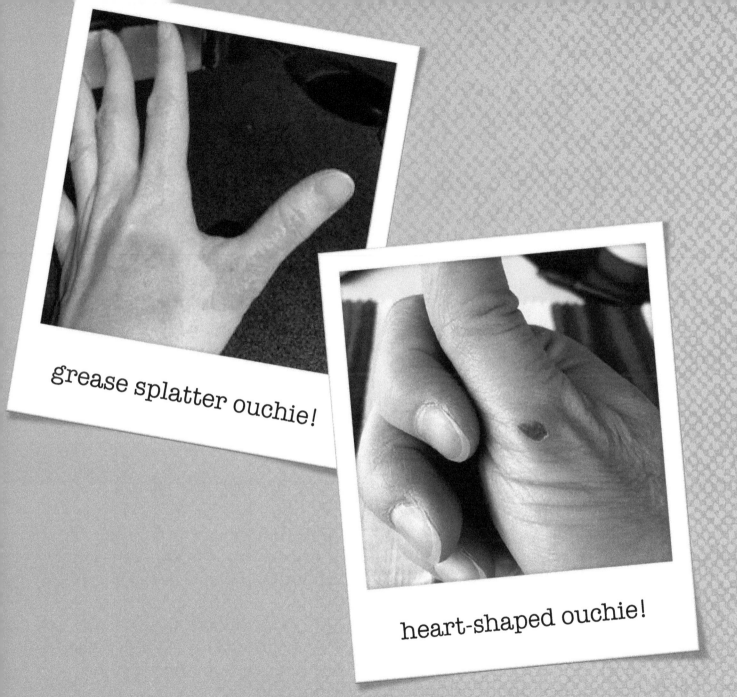

grease splatter ouchie!

heart-shaped ouchie!

225

Leslie Hart-Davidson

The crock pot is my super favorite cooking tool. The variety of glorious gastronomical goodies it can produce is just stunning—everything from super complicated fare to crazy easy dinners. This recipe has a veg and a few fancy herbs in it, but you could literally dump a five dollah whole chicken in a wide crock pot with 2 cups of water and come home to a delicious meal. Let's not overthink this.

1 whole thawed chicken, 5-7lbs
4 carrots, cut into veggie
tray-style chunks
(2 cups of bagged baby
carrots are cool too)
4-6 sprigs thyme
3-4 sprigs rosemary
1 C chicken stock
1 C water
Salt & Pepper

Directions

In a wide crock pot, create a bed of carrots on the bottom and lay the rosemary and thyme on top. Open the chicken in your sink and yank out any innards still stuffed inside. Drain any extra liquid from the cavity, then put clucky to rest on the carrot bed breast side up. Pour the liquid over top, then grind fresh pepper over the bird until your arms hurt. Finally, add salt and cover the crock. Cook on high for 4 hours, then turn to warm until you're ready to eat. You can also do low heat for 6-8 hours.

Clucky will be fall-aparty when it's done cooking. Use tongs or a big fork to place the big chunks on a plate. You can serve the chunks with the side of carrots as is, or you can process the chicken into delicious meaty parts to use in salads, casseroles, quesadillas, or protein bowls. The chicken bits will stay safe in a covered dish in the fridge for several days, or frozen in baggies for a few months.

puppers love
leftover carrots
on dry kibble

Yields: 6 servings
Pairs with: a quick YouTube watch of the Anal Retentive Chef from SNL.
Consideration: So damn easy.

I was a complete mealtime asshole around age 5. I demanded a segmented plate with dividers so my food wouldn't touch. I insisted upon using the special tiny fork that my mother had graciously stolen for me from Red Lobster. I crossed my little arms in defiance and wouldn't eat if I didn't like what was being served. "Karma," my mother would say. Mama used to cry in the 1940's when her older sister cut her toast wrong in the morning and would demand that she make her new pieces, so mama considered my picky mealtime behavior retribution for her own childhood culinary transgressions. I grew out of that phase once I gained enough self-awareness to realize that I was inconveniencing my mama for no good reason. Annnnd also when I went to dinner at a friend's house and watched my pal's brother get his ass whooped for refusing a burger from Wendy's because it had pickles on it. Ohhh, parenting in the 70's.

All of us are picky in some way, so I want to address a very specific kind of pickiness that relates to cooking. Let's rule out one thing first: if you have specific food allergies rather than aversions, you're excused from this tirade. Please jump ahead to the "Can't Touch That" section. I also want to excuse food restrictors from this section. Many folks are labeled "picky eaters" when in fact they have religious, political, ethical or health reasons for not consuming certain categories of food. That's not what this section is about. I want to address the people that cross their arms in defiance and sneer when food touches on the plate or the presentation isn't *just so*. I have one message for you: fuck you. You're not special.

If you haven't tossed this book across the room out of frustration from reading the last line, I'll explain why I just leveled judgment. Whether the fussy epicurean is your partner, kid(s) or a dinner guest, picky eaters are a monumental pain in the ass for the cook. Here's an example of a dinner I once prepared for a group of friends and family who were picky eaters: the main dish was my famous next level mac and cheese (see pg 234). The contents include onion, broccoli and bias-sliced smoked holiday kielbasa from the butcher that are all gently sautéed, then reduced with chicken stock to impart more flavor. I carefully layer the macaroni with shredded cheese and the sautéed mix, then place beautifully sliced roma tomatoes on top before repeating the process. The béchamel sauce is drizzled over the casserole and the whole dish is topped with tons of shredded cheese before baking. It's a beautiful, tasty THING.

My guests, however, insisted on a few modifications that they were unwilling to work around. One despised broccoli and all vegetable matter. The other refused to pick out the dastardly tomatoes and wanted a "clean" casserole. The last, my picky pain-in-the-ass kid who eats nothing, just wanted the macaroni noodles, but cooked in chicken stock and with tons of butter and Parmesan cheese.

I ended up making 4 separate meals that evening to accommodate the picky requests of my guests who were not quick to thank me for the extra effort and still eyed the dish suspiciously looking for unwanted vegetable matter. Was it a chore? Hell yes. It took me twice as long, and that damn casserole (while I absolutely love it) takes more than an hour to assemble. So why did I do it? Because food is love.

I realize I'm not making a good argument here for why Picktastic Putter-Offers should cook for the food-challenged. It was a ton of work to make that 4-part dinner happen, but it was only one night out of my life. I want to

Leslie Hart-Davidson

offer ways that everyday cooks can cope with having picky family members so that you don't want to shove a fork in your eye or whoop some ass every time you hear "eww!"

1. Name those neuroses

"Let's get to the bottom of this!" is one of my favorite quotes from my business manager Jen. Grab a pen, paper and the picky eater, then ask them to list all the foods that they love at the very top of the page. Beneath that, draw a vertical line down the middle to create two columns. The left column lists all the foods that are (literally) off the table for them. Tomatoes? Broccoli? Pizza? Whatever it is, list it. To the right of each eww item, have the picky eater write why they hate that item. Is it the flavor? The texture? Some sort of combo? Force the picky eater to be very specific about describing the eww-inducing nature of each item.

Being able to list the eww items and thinking carefully about the reasoning behind each reaction will not only help the picky eater better understand the categories of eww, but also help discover potential new food items or combinations to try that would be agreeable to the whole family.

2. Enforce picky eater participation

Insisting that the picky person contribute to the meal in some fashion is a proactive way to get more buy-in from them and create a positive outcome. There are three distinct ways to become part of the front-end process: menu prep, shopping, and actual cooking. First, have the picky eater plan a menu for the week with meals that are manageable and adaptable for the whole family. This will help prevent nightly fights when the picky eater sits down to dinner and can't find a damn thing to say "eww" about since they're the ones who selected the meal. Second, have the picky eater accompany you to the grocery to select the menu items and have a good look-see at other foods that strike their fancy. It's a great opportunity to expose the picky eater to other options that are similar to ones they already enjoy and start conversations about food and cooking. Finally, have the picky eater assist you in the kitchen with meal prep and cooking. Assign tasks based on their age and skill level that will help them better understand the process of cooking and how much effort is involved. It might be as simple as just fetching items from the refrigerator and panty for you, or perhaps you hand over the cutting board and knife. Ask the picky eater what part of the cooking process they're most interested in and go from there. Sometimes, having the picky eater experience food in the context of creation rather than presentation can change their attitude of pickiness (crosses fingers).

3. **Offer create-your-own meals**

I'm not talking about "fending," which is a term both my nieces use when their folks just don't cook that day. "When it gets to be about 7:30 and nobody's in the kitchen, I'll just grab a can of ravioli or a bowl of cereal," one niece explained. Fending for yourself when there's no specific meal planned is different from the create-your-own version that I'm recommending for picky eaters. In this scenario, there's a base food that you build with different items that are on the side. Pasta and homemade pizza are excellent examples of customizable foods. You could serve pasta with sauce and have meatballs, cheese, fungus, or other veggies on the side for each person to add in. Individual steamed packets of frozen vegetables are a quick fix that don't even require an extra pan, so the effort is minimal. The pizza is just as easy. Ready-made pizza crust or small pieces of naan are great for making individual pizzas, and most ingredients like pepperoni and cheese come right out of a package that don't require a ton of prep. Everybody is eating relatively the same thing and still gets exactly what they want.

Wrap your brain around this for me, because I haven't been able to: my kid won't eat my food. My brilliant, lovely, badass, fearless, awesome teenage daughter flat-out refuses to eat anything other than shit that comes out of a box. You feel my pain, right? A kid born to foodie parents who dislikes eating is quite a brain-bender.

Luckily, the kid knows her way around the kitchen pretty well. Once we had our food truce established and stopped fighting about not partaking in dinner, I told the kid she was on her own. "I'm not making two separate meals," I explained, "so I'll teach you how to fend for yourself."

stubborn kid pasta
i'll sneak some protein in somehow.

⅓ C dried orzo
1 14.5 oz can reduced sodium chicken stock (or 2 C)
1 TB butter
2 tsp grated parmesan cheese

In a pan, bring the stock to a boil over high heat. Add the orzo and reduce the heat to medium high. Keep a close eye on the orzo, stirring frequently and adjusting the heat so that the pan has a good boil but doesn't foam at the top. Cook for about 9 minutes, stirring often until the orzo is tender and the liquid evaporates. Pull the pan from the heat and add a pat of butter. Stir and serve in the kid's favorite bowl, topping with "shaky cheese" if desired.

Note: When substituting other pasta shapes, the dry measurement becomes ½ cup and the package directions for cooking times may vary. The stock might not evaporate so strain before adding butter.

Yields: 1 serving
Pairs with: the smug satisfaction that you were NEVER an asshole as a kid.
Consideration: adults love it, too.

the bedrooms
of teens are
burial grounds
for dishes

233

Much like Jim Hart's meatballs, next level mac & cheese is a labor of love thanks to multiple steps and the quantity of dishes dirtied. I originally learned this recipe from Mama Mace, my bestie's mom in New York. I've played with the ingredients over the years to see how next level I could truly make it. I promise that the incredible flavor and texture of this dish will be well worth the effort!

8 oz macaroni
4 heads broccoli, chopped into bite-sized pieces (about 6 cups)
2 links smoked kielbasa, sliced on the bias
1 large yellow onion
2 TB evoo
3-4 roma tomatoes, sliced
¼ C chicken stock
3 C grated sharp cheddar cheese

Béchamel
2 TB Butter
½ tsp salt
½ tsp pepper
¼ C flour
1 ½ C milk

Preheat the oven to 425 degrees. Cook macaroni according to package instructions until al dente but not overdone. Drain and set aside. While the pasta is cooking, steam the broccoli in a shallow microwave safe dish with about an inch of water in it. Cover with plastic wrap and nuke it for 4ish minutes. (It's cool if you need to split it in two batches.) Drain carefully and set aside.

In a big pan, heat the evoo and sauté the onions on medium high heat until translucent, about 3 minutes. Add the drained broccoli and stir to incorporate the evoo. Sauté until the onions are golden, about 5 minutes. Toss in the sliced kielbasa, then increase the heat to high and grind some fresh pepper until your arms hurt.

234

(continued on next page)

Yields: 6 servings
Pairs with: a salad to atone for the many bad calories.
Consideration: even better as leftovers.

Stir frequently and allow to cook for another 2-3 minutes. When the pan looks dry, splash in the chicken stock and scrape up any brown bits. Continue to cook until the stock evaporates for a couple more minutes, then remove from heat and set aside.

Before you make the béchamel, make an assembly line with the pan of sautéed goodness, cheese, salt & pepper, macaroni and sliced tomatoes. Grab a rectangular 9 x 13 Pyrex pan and place it central to all the ingredients.

It's béchamel time. Don't be frightened of the mother sauces. You got this, boo. One rule: DON'T WALK AWAY. Never leave your béchamel, k? Not even to the people you'd choose as guardians of your small children. Wait, there are two rules: GET YOUR SHIT TOGETHER BEFORE YOU START. In a small saucepan over medium heat, melt butter. Doooon't let it brown. Brown butter sucks donkey balls and you'll have to start over. When the butter is all melty, plop in the flour, salt and pepper. Whisk until combined. It's totally fine if it all globs into the center of the whisk—the little guys are just having a fat and protein party in the center. Break it up by gently tapping the whisk on the side of the pan to knock it all out. Sing to it, if you'd like: "You don't have to go home, but you can't stay here."

Milk time! Pour it in the pan and get ready to whisk to break up the fat and protein party. Careful not to sploosh the milk over the side of the pan (burned milk stinks to high heaven and is no fun to clean up.)

Here's the magic part: turn up the heat a bit to medium flirting with high and keep whisking. You'll feel a change in texture after about 2 minutes, so don't stop stirring. Your béchamel is ready when it's juuuust past the consistency of pancake batter. Think more along the lines of Mod Podge than sausage gravy. You want to be able to ladle it on top of the macaroni, so pull it when you find that sweet spot (huhuhuh TWSS.)

It's layering o'clock! Begin with half of the cooked macaroni as the bottom layer. Spread it evenly and sprinkle on salt and pepper. Place half of the sautéed goodies over top, then space half the roma tomato slices in about 3 rows roughly near the center of each serving piece. There's no wrong placement if you like tomatoes; just plop them on evenly.

Top with ribbons of half of the béchamel, then sprinkle on one cup of cheese. Repeat the layer with macaroni, seasonings, sautéed bits and tomatoes. Press down the layers with a spatula. Add the remaining béchamel, then top the whole kit and kaboodle with two cups of cheese.

Cover with nonstick foil and bake for 40 minutes. Remove foil and brown the top cheese with the broiler if you'd like. Allow to cool for 10-15 minutes if you can stand it.

237

Leslie Hart-Davidson

Nothing ruins dinner faster than anaphylaxis. When I invite new guests to the Compound for dinner, I always start with an important question: "Any food allergies or sensitivities? Any possible way I could kill you with a meal?" Even if my main menu plans didn't include any potential allergens that a guest names, it's helpful to know so I can be on the lookout with all of my ingredients. I learned this the hard way after my business manager Jen who has Hoshimoto's disease was diagnosed with a gluten allergy. I cook for Jen as part of her compensation package, so I had to learn quickly that "cut out the gluten" isn't as simple as "don't serve pasta or bread." Jen called my slip-ups "being glufied" when I would cook with items that had gluten lurking deep in the ingredient list. Soy sauce, bbq sauce, and cans of beef stock were among my first few mistakes, causing her some nasty side effects. Oops.

Allergies are no small matter. According to the USDA (United States Department of Agriculture) Food Safety and Inspection Service, "While more than 160 foods can cause allergic reactions in people with food allergies, the Food Allergen Labeling and Consumer Protection Act (FALCPA) has identified the eight most common allergenic foods. These eight foods account for 90 percent of food allergic reactions. They are: milk, eggs, fish (such as bass, flounder, cod), crustacean shellfish (such as crab, lobster, shrimp), tree nuts (such as almonds, walnuts, pecans), peanuts, wheat, and soybeans. These eight, and any ingredient that contains protein derived from one or more of them, are designated as "major food allergens" by the FALCPA, which was passed by Congress in 2004 and became effective in 2006."

Whether you or your family members are newly diagnosed with a food sensitivity or allergy or you've been coping with it for a hot minute, here are some strategies to help keep everyone healthy and safe during meals:

1. **Know the severity**

   There's a difference between a food sensitivity and a full-out allergy: the former can inconvenience you, the latter can kill you. Having full knowledge of the potential reaction is important so you understand how diligent you need to be with preparation and cooking at home. If certain airborne food particles can cause an allergic reaction, for example, it's best to never have those items in your pantry or refrigerator. If the severity is less, then keep those ingredients separate during cooking and be sure to use coded utensils, cutting boards and pans. When I make Jen's gluten-free pasta dishes alongside my regular pasta, I have a special pan and spoon that are only used for her meals. She even has designated bakeware ramekins that make her squeal when she sees them. "My own special dish!" she'll yell. "I'm SPECIAL!!!!" She sure is.

2. **Read food labels super carefully**

   Potential allergens are hiding everywhere and sometimes masquerade as different things. Using the gluten issue as an example again, I mistook the lack of the word "wheat" in the labeling as a safe product when it actually contained malt. If you're newly diagnosed with an allergy, ask your doctor for a consultation with a nutritionist to better understand how to keep yourself safe. There are also many parent-centered allergy support groups that can make your child's food experiences better. The National Institute of Allergy and Infectious Diseases (NIAID), a part of the National Institutes of Health (NIH), is a great resource for educating yourself on safely interpreting labels and keeping everyone free from unintentional ingestion.

Leslie Hart-Davidson

3. Know it's a process

For newly diagnosed issues, it'll take time to figure out how to navigate your kitchen using menu substitutions or omitting ingredients completely. Over time, you'll figure out if you need to rearrange your prep space or invest in new tools like cutting boards that are only to be used for certain foods, or drawers in the fridge that contain safe snacks. Whatever system you develop for your family, be sure to thoroughly explain the what-goes-where rules that everyone can follow. It's also a process to learn ingredient substitutions for favorite meals, so don't beat yourself up like I did when I tried and failed at my first gluten free béchamel (which was total wallpaper paste). Do some recipe research and get advice on adaptations from others in the allergy community so that you can continue to enjoy your favorite meals risk-free.

Can't Touch That

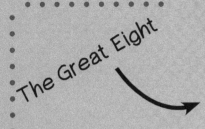

The Great Eight

Milk	Tree Nuts
Eggs	Peanuts
Fish	Wheat
Shellfish	Soybeans

The FDA.gov website for food allergens has a wealth of knowledge about package labeling to keep consumers safe with their food selections. In 2004, the Food Allergen Labeling and Consumer Protection Act (FALCPA) was passed to protect the 30,000 Americans a year who required emergency room treatment for adverse food reactions.

There are two ways that allergens must appear on a food label:

1. In parentheses following the name of the ingredient

   Flour (wheat)

   Whey (milk)

2. As a "contains" list next to or immediately after the ingredients

   "Contains milk, soy, and wheat"

Leslie Hart-Davidson

Comfort food is a total THING. Jim Hart would create this lovely loaf weekly during Midwest winters when I was little, and it's one of my prized hand-written recipes that he gave me when I graduated college and set up my own home. Though originally bread-tastic, I adapted the recipe to be gluten-free by substituting Rice Krispies. This blue plate special is best served with crack mashed taties and peas, though any of your favorite veg will work.

jim hart's meatloaf
cook 'til it's done.

2 lbs fresh ground beef (90% lean)
3 cups Rice Krispies
2 eggs
2 TB horseradish
1 tsp garlic powder
2 tsp salt
2 tsp ground pepper
1 cup ketchup plus 2 TBS
1 small onion, finely diced
1 small green pepper, finely diced
3 stalks celery, finely diced
2 TB Worchestershire

Yields: 6 servings
Pairs with: blue plates and Parks and Rec reruns.
Consideration: makes for a killer sandwich.

Preheat oven to 400 degrees. In a large bowl, whisk the two eggs along with horseradish. Dice the onion, green bell pepper and celery, then toss in the egg mixture. Plop in the ground beef and sprinkle on the garlic powder, salt and pepper. Add 2 tablespoons of ketchup along with the Worchestershire sauce.

If you're squicked out by touching raw meat, grab a plastic glove or a large plastic storage baggie and shove your hand inside like a haphazard food condom. Mix the crap out of the beef goo until you're confident that the mixture is blended (or until your hand hurts. Either one.)

(continued on next page)

the finer the dice,
the better it holds
together

243

Add the Rice Krispies one cup at a time and mush again with the baggie condom until blended or your hand-claw spasms.

Grab a 9 x13 Pyrex baking dish and plop half of the beef goo in the Pyrex to one side. Mold the goo like a flattened oblong football-ish shape so that it can cook evenly. Repeat and place both footballs in the Pyrex. Squirt each loaf with enough ketchup to completely cover the top (about 1 cup) and finish with a sprinkling of ground pepper.

Cover the top of the Pyrex pan with foil and bake for roughly 45 minutes until cooked through. Remove the loaves to a plate and allow to cool for about 5 minutes before you slice it and present the butts to the most favored family member. Jim Hart's meatloaf is also excellent as leftovers sliced on sandwiches.

James Dean-era Jim Hart

Jim Hart at granddaughter
Lily's baby shower

Leslie Hart-Davidson

Downhill

Immediately following the build-up of the Star Wars viewing, Greg started to feel significant pain. This is the guy that never took more than Tylenol after major surgery, so I knew that if he was asking for something stronger, he had to be pretty bad off. We feared that the chemo drug wasn't as effective as we hoped and that the tumor was growing. The oncologist wanted to wait a full two months before rescanning to check the tumor and it wasn't quite time yet. Despite the pain, Greg still didn't complain. "'I'm ok," he'd say when I checked on him. He slept a ton and was moving slower, but his attitude was still positive. He talked frequently about how happy it made him to think about getting back to work and being productive again. "I feel bad for my coworkers taking on my route and doing so much extra," he said. "I just want to go to work."

The first week in February, I arrived at my brother's to take him to an appointment. "Sit down," he said hoarsely. "I'm not okay. Something's wrong. I can't go the appointment. I need you to call an ambulance." The paramedics arrived quickly and helped my brother to the hospital. The attending physician immediately called The James Cancer Center and arranged a transfer to their hospital for better care. Even while in the ER, Greg continued to be polite and kind to the medical staff. "How are you?" they'd ask. "I'm ok," he'd whisper. "Well, obviously not if you're in the ER," the doctor jokingly replied. When the transport team arrived to take him to The James, Greg was trying to help them move his backpack and belongings. "Sir, how about you let us do that for you?" they told him.

At The James, the intake team poked and prodded Greg and asked a zillion questions. It was harder for him to speak that day, so as I often did, I became his voice and rattled off every detail necessary to fill in the picture for the doctors. I'd frequently look back at Greg for clarification and confirmation as I answered new questions. He'd nod, then mouth "thank you" when the interview was complete.

Food is Love

The next day after all the scans and tests, the oncology team pulled me out to the hallway to deliver the news. "First, there's fluid around his heart which is causing the breathing issues. More importantly, the chemo protocol didn't work at all," they began. "In fact, his tumor growth has accelerated so much that it fractured his vertebrae. There's absolutely nothing we can do other than make him comfortable. We're so sorry."

Mama had prepared me in September, so I knew what was coming. I walked back into my brother's room and gently broke the news to him. "You fought really hard for a long time," I told him as bravely as I could. "The tumor won." "It's over?" he asked. "Yeah." "Well, fuck." Greg replied, then closed his eyes to sleep again.

Keep something in mind for me: "Well, fuck" was the most that Greg had ever said about his diagnosis, prognosis or general condition since September 19th. There were never, ever any moments of "why me?" or "maybe I shoulda" that ever entered our conversations. Never. I'll tell you that Greg was not in denial about the severity of the situation; he simply chose not to give his energy to the subjunctive.

Part of my other responsibility during this caregiving process was managing the expectations of friends and family. Greg didn't want visitors as it caused him physical pain to have to entertain them, and after chemotherapy started, it was dangerous for others to bring their germs into his home. I would Silkwood myself before entering and clean the shit out of his apartment before I left to make sure he was okay. As a trade-off for not being able to visit him, the concerned friends and family would call me to get updates. I would patiently explain the next steps and last doctor visits in minimal detail at my brother's request. When Greg was admitted to The James in February, I encountered the biggest onslaught of subjunctive abuse in my life.

249

Leslie Hart-Davidson

What's subjunctive abuse? It's the equivalent of Monday morning quarterbacking. Each person I spoke with would listen as I delivered the upsetting news about Greg's tumor, then proceed from a place of both great love and concern to tell me what I SHOULD have done to improve my brother's chances or what he COULD have done years ago to get early treatment or what I OUGHT to do right now. Each time I listened to all those subjunctive suggestions during a call, I would close my eyes and refer to the script I had rehearsed. "I don't have a time machine, so we're stuck with the reality of the present. Our reality is that he received the very best treatment possible in the country at The James and that he is being cared for exceptionally well at the moment. But thanks for your advice."

My brother Greg, the kindest, gentlest, most grateful person I knew, died peacefully in his sleep at The James on February 7th having never used the subjunctive to define his illness.

1970's space nerd Greg

LHD learns gaming from Greg

Greg's 7th birthday

251

Leslie Hart-Davidson

two litte mice

"One, two, three, fourrrrr, FIVE!" I felt the cold shiny pennies drop in my tiny hand as Mom counted out the coins. She told my brother and me to hustle as we entered the Upper Valley mall in search of Halloween costumes. Our first stop at the mall was always to the main fountain so I could throw in my coins and make wishes. "Hurry up!" Greg yelled. "I want to get my Darth Vader costume before they sell out!"

I intentionally took my time throwing in the coins, wishing for the jerky kid in my class to quit hogging the Spirograph during playtime, and for the coolest Peanuts Lucy costume I can find, and for my big brother to like me, need me, and want to hang out with me. I finished my coin chucking, then caught up to my family.

On the way to the costume store, I lingered at a kiosk where a lady with long dark hair and thick glasses was doing custom artwork. She looked just like a cartoon lady on a Schoolhouse Rock episode. "I see two little mice!" she said, her eyes darting between my brother and me. Mom was tickled by the idea of sweet mice made from thumbprints on an oval resin plaque. "What's your name, sweetness?" she asked me. "LC," I said, staring at the thumbprint art and reveling in the creativity. "I can put you and your brother on a plaque together. Would you like that?" I smiled and looked at Mom. She and the artist negotiated a price, and I turned to Greg with much anticipation. "We're going to be mice together!" I told him, expecting as much joy in return. Instead, Greg huffed. "This is dumb. I don't want to be a dumb mouse and have a dumb thumbprint with you. I just want my Darth Vader costume!"

Mom raised her left eyebrow as high as the Empire State building and eyeballed my brother. He stared at the terrazzo floor and studied each speck remorsefully while the artist prepared the ink for the thumbprint. I offered up my tiny hand to the long-haired lady. She carefully rolled my thumb in ink, then pressed it into the plaque. Greg sighed, then offered up his thumb to repeat the process. He made quite a show of rubbing his thumb on his jeans to remove the ink. Greg watched as the artist drew little tails and ears and such on the thumbprints. "You're not going to show this to people, are you?" Greg asked Mom. Exasperated, she huffed "I'm going to put this in the kitchen for the next 30 years for EVERYONE to see!"

Greg turned to me and scowled. "You owe me," he said. "My friends are going to make fun of me for this and I might not get my Darth Vader costume!" I felt awful for delaying the shopping trip and risking the Vader acquisition, but I was secretly thrilled that I had something in my tiny five-year-old hand that put my brother right next to me. My wish was coming true, even if it was in rodent form.

Greg found his Vader costume that afternoon. I settled for Woodstock since Lucy Van Pelt wasn't available. We went home and Mom hung the mouse plaque in the kitchen as promised, taunting my brother for not being nice to me.

The thumb mice hung in Mom's kitchen for exactly 31 years before she died and I inherited the plaque. It now lives in my kitchen.

A few days ago, Greg and I received the devastating news that his tumor hadn't responded to the chemotherapy treatment. Instead, it continued growing to epic proportions and is now life-threatening. For the past five months, I have been paying my karmic debt plus interest for the indignity of making him create a thumbprint mouse. The roughly million percent interest is worth it, though, because ultimately my penny wish in the Upper Valley mall fountain came true: my big brother likes me, needs me and wants to hang out with me now.

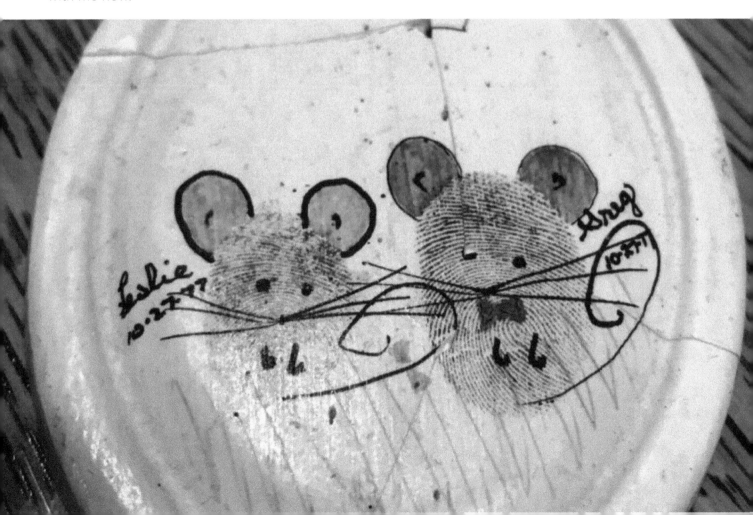

M y pal Nate is a quality human and an outstanding cook, but his sense of humor is what I appreciate most about him. In the thick of my brother travels, Nate was kind enough leave a pan of this ridonkulously tasty emergency lasagna on my porch with note stating "for use when too much life is happening." I guarantee this recipe is fabulous in any life scenario, so please enjoy!

1 TB evoo
½ lb ground chuck
½ lb ground pork
1 C red wine
1 C low sodium chicken stock
2-3 bay leaves
1 28 oz can tomato puree
1 tsp dried oregano
1 tsp dried basil
1 tsp fennel seeds
16 oz tub ricotta cheese
¼ tsp freshly grated nutmeg
(fresh is SO much better)
1 ½ lbs low-moisture whole-
milk mozzarella
½ cup Romano
9 lasagna noodles
Salt and pepper to taste

Directions

In a large pan, brown the ground meats in evoo at medium high heat. Mush the meaty bits into a fine consistency and cook until thoroughly browned and sizzling. Turn the heat to high and add the wine. Cook off the alcohol rapidly and lower the heat to a simmer. Add chicken broth and bay leaves, then simmer for 10 minutes. Toss in the tomato puree, oregano, basil and fennel seeds and give it a swish. Simmer on low for 45 minutes, adding broth or water if the sauce becomes too thick to spread. Fish out the bay leaves, add salt and pepper to taste, then divide into fourths for the lasagna layers.

While the sauce is on its last simmer, boil a giant pot of salted water and cook the 9 lasagna noodles for half of the recommended package direction time. Drain and return to the pot with room temperature water until you're ready to build the lasagna.

Yields: 6 servings
Pairs with: a calamity or sad-ness.
Consideration: easy to over-eat, so cut small portions.

leftovers are
just as divine

Whip up the ricotta by grabbing a bowl and mixing the 16 oz tub with freshly grated nutmeg, then set aside. Grate the giant chunks of mozzarella and romano cheese, keeping them in separate piles.

Preheat oven to 375 degrees and dust off the part of your brain that holds fractions. In a 9 x 13 baking pan, add the first ¼ bloop of sauce to the bottom and swoosh it around. Lay three noodles down and equally distribute the next ¼ bloop of sauce across the noodles. Carefully spread ½ of the ricotta mixture (a cake icing spatula works well), then add ⅓ of the mozzarella and ⅓ of the romano cheeses. Sprinkle with dried oregano. Repeat this layer starting with noodles, then sauce, remaining ricotta, grated cheeses and dried oregano. For the final layer, top the noodles with sauce and remaining shredded cheeses followed by a final sprinkle of oregano.

Bake covered with foil for 45 minutes, then remove foil and continue baking for 15ish minutes until the top is golden brown and bubbling. Allow the emergency lasagna to rest for 15-20 minutes before serving.

Nate's note about emergency lasagna

Food is Love

Plate Collection

Visceral memories of my childhood pop up for me frequently. Anything can trigger it—a color, a scent, a sound—and I'm transported to a time and place to relive that experience. One of my most intense visceral memories was at age 4 in my living room sitting on a scratchy Early American textured sofa with my brother Greg. We were eating dinner on tv trays in our jammies. The smell of the grill still lingered as I took bites of my burger and French fries from the round, mildly lipped brown plate. I loved how I could chase the ketchup around the edge of it without spilling over. I loved that the color was the same as my favorite m&m.

I paid much attention to dinnerware after that when I discovered that not all plates were created equally. My grandmother had heavily patterned plates from Germany that she used for Sunday dinner. I liked swirling around the gravy to uncover the scenes below. My neighbors had Corelle, which has a texture that I have never, ever liked. The oval shape of restaurant breakfast plates always intrigued me. I've never ignored a plate in my life.

I learned to love plates as a bigger symbol of the effort put forth during a meal. I've amassed such a plate collection that I had to buy more furniture to store them. I am the Imelda Marcos of dinnerware. In my defense, I use every single one of the dozens of place settings I've accumulated over the years. Whenever there is an opportunity with plating to show more care and love for your people, an opportunity to Give, I highly recommend you do it. You never know whose visceral memory you'll influence.

257

Leslie Hart-Davidson

crap

When I remodeled my own kitchen in 2018, I called upon every bit of design knowledge from my 20+ year career to make the best decisions for layout, lighting and finish selections in the new space. During the design phase, I user-tested all of my intended changes during nightly cooking to ensure that the new plan would be functional as well as stunning.

The kitchens I create for my clients undergo the same process of design and testing to find the best-looking functional space. Many clients come to me after a deep dive into HGTV to find a kitchen that they'd like to reproduce. "It's pretty," they'll say. "I can't tell you why I like it; it just feels good to look at. All the finishes go together and that's what I want."

This lack of language to be able to specifically describe the desired elements that make "great" space is a giant roadblock to successful design. In my first book *Remodeling Your House without Killing Your Spouse*, I introduced the concept of CRAP, a design language. CRAP is an acronym that stands for Contrast, Repetition, Alignment and Proximity. It provides a vocabulary to better communicate your feelings, diagnose a space when something isn't right, and treat the space to a glow-up so that it feels and functions as best it can.

It is the presence and balance of these four CRAP elements that allow a user to feel harmony, happiness, contentment and functionality within a room. Think of the concept as a more sciency version of feng shui and you'll get the hang of it.

Food is Love

Let's take a look at each of the four CRAP elements using my remodeled farm kitchen to see how impactful they are in the overall design.

contrast

repetition

alignment

proximity

 CRAP is developed from *The Non-Designer's Design Book* by digital goddess Robin Williams who wrote about two-dimensional graphic and web design.

Leslie Hart-Davidson

texture for days

The original 1870's exposed brick provides excellent contrast in texture when paired with modern black stainless appliances

ballsy color

High color contrast emanates from the ballsy black paint above the stark white window trim. The antiqued blue tall corner cabinet provides more color contrast from the wood stained base cabinets.

Food is Love

crap

contrast

Contrast highlights the differences between finishes in the kitchen to show visual interest. Too little contrast is a snoozefest, and too much contrast is visually jarring. There are three ways to achieve contrast in a room: color, texture and size. Let's take a look at how each element impacts the overall look and functionality of a kitchen.

COLOR
TEXTURE
SIZE

size matters

The black and white vinyl composition flooring tiles are a contrasting scale in the connecting rooms: 2'x2' squares in the large open kitchen and 1' square tiles in the smaller butler's pantry beautifully highlight the size difference.

261

Leslie Hart-Davidson

70/30 rule in action

The "Starbucks" seating area of the Compound kitchen is a good example of balanced thematic elements. The grouping of 4 chairs would be overkill if all were the same style and color, and head-scratching if all were completely different seating. The combination of two colors and two chair styles is a happy medium that asserts a theme without screaming or whispering "hey, look at me!"

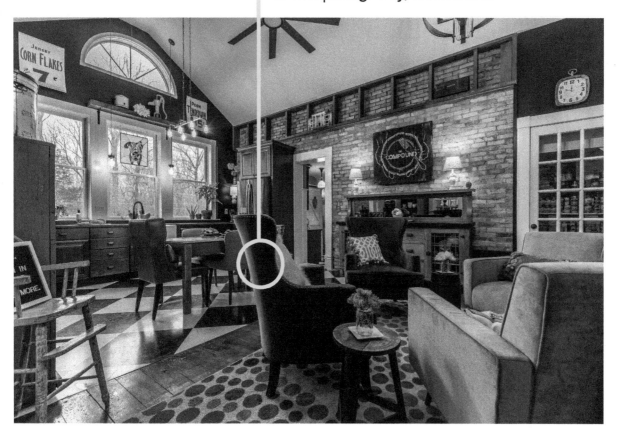

Food is Love

crap

repetition

Repetition asserts a theme through multiples. "Theme" can be interpreted in many ways: a style, a genre, or a look—it doesn't matter what you call it; your eye will search for the common elements within the kitchen and try to make sense of the story you're trying to tell. Warning: themes are for parties, not for rooms! Make sure to follow the 70/30 rule when it comes to themed décor and strive to keep the theme-y bits to a happy 50% range.

The 70/30 rule applies to all of the thematic elements in a room: décor, artwork, colors, furnishings and architecture. If more than 70% of those elements are linked in a specific theme, it's like being beaten over the head with the idea. Conversely, if fewer than 30% of the thematic elements are linked, you give a big "HUH?!?!?!" to the space because it doesn't tell a cohesive or compelling story. Keeping the thematic elements to 50% provides proper balance.

263

Leslie Hart-Davidson

zero Indiana-ing effect

The spacing and height of the vintage grocery sale signs, antique beam with memorabilia and the derpy dog stained glass allows the eye to rest on an object before flowing to the next treasure.

crap

alignment

Alignment shows hierarchy through placement. Much like animal pack law, some things are just more important than others. Your eyes are constantly seeking the alpha element in a room and will be hella-disappointed if the hierarchy of décor isn't easily identifiable. The goal with alignment is to allow your eye to stop and rest in appreciation of an element before moving on to the next visual cue.

There are two forms of alignment to avoid: the *Indiana effect* and the *Royal Caribbean effect*. Indiana-ing involves forcing the eye to travel in a straight line while viewing artwork or architectural elements all presented at the same height. The effect is the same as driving through the flat Midwest state: your eye zips past mundane and uninspiring scenery. Yes, I'm allowed to say that. I lived in Indiana for five years.

Royal Caribbean-ing involves the opposite strategy: placing artwork and elements here and there and hither and yon so that your eye bobs up and down around the space like a seasick cruise line passenger. Tossing your cookies is never a thing in design, so keep your eyes happy by allowing them to stop and rest before moving on to the next cool thing.

265

Leslie Hart-Davidson

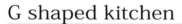

single wall kitchen

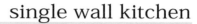

The Single Wall kitchen has a super squishy triangle shape. You won't get your 10,000 daily steps in this configuration, but you might feel like you're in a cue for an amusement park ride with all the back-and-forth.

While the overall layout is pretty simplistic, the single wall kitchen can be super efficient if the counter space between the appliances is ample for safely landing your food and cookware.

G shaped kitchen

The G-Shaped kitchen has a traditionally even triangle shape. The hook of the "G" is created by a peninsula which serves as the barrier to too much interior traffic. The peninsula seating outside the main triangle allows for social visitation, light prepwork assistance and casual dining without bumping butts with the cook.

This G-Shape is essentially a 'roided up U-shaped kitchen that can be super efficient for introverted or dictatorial cooks who need you to stay out of their damn way.

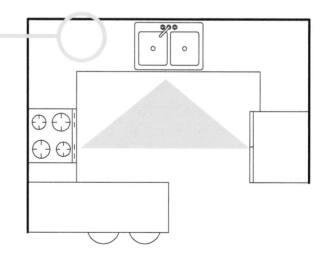

266

crap

proximity

WORK
TRIANGLES

In the world of two-dimensional design, proximity is defined as showing similarity among sets of items though location. In the real world, it's really all about function. Stuff's gotta work, or no amount of pretty will cover the dysfunction. You can knock yourself out creating the perfect contrast, beautiful repetition and the most amazing alignment you've ever seen. Warning: if your kitchen doesn't function, you have failed like McDonald's pizza.

The concept of proximity in kitchen design is often expressed through the work triangle—that cool three-point relationship between the stove, refrigerator and sink. No matter what shape your kitchen layout is, the size and shape of the triangle determines the proximal efficiency. Let's look at kitchen layout styles to better understand proximity.

Leslie Hart-Davidson

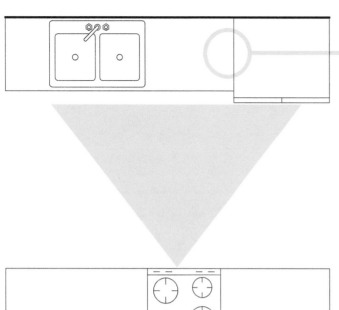

galley wall kitchen

The Galley Wall kitchen has a deeper triangle shape that is famous for butt-bumping if more than one cook is in the kitchen. This layout is common in apartments and ranch homes and has the potential to break noses and inflict goose eggs on unwitting residents who walk into the open fridge while turning the blind corner.

Given how short the triangle sides are, the efficiency of the galley kitchen with a single user is pretty high.

L shaped kitchen

The L-Shaped kitchen has a long, narrow triangle shape that's conducive to multiple cooks. The openness of the triangle allows for two users to be positioned so that one can pass around the backside without bumping butts or dropping dishes.

Overall, the L-shaped kitchen is most efficient if the longest leg of the triangle does not exceed 9'.

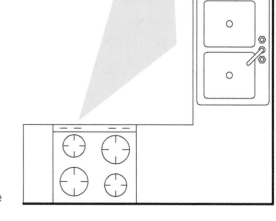

268

island feature kitchen

The Island Feature kitchen has a wedged triangle shape that allows the cook to perform culinary ballet with elegant turns, twirls and strides to get to each appliance. This layout is useful for multiple prep spots, so more than one cook can access the space.

Unlike the Galley style, the island offers escape routes on either side to prevent butt-bumping the cook. Overall, the efficiency of the Island Feature kitchen is high.

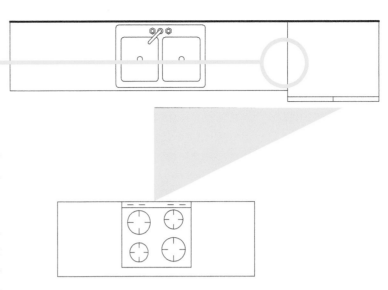

U shaped kitchen

The U-Shaped kitchen has a wide, even triangle shape that functions like an oval racetrack. Each lap takes the cook efficiently around the appliances with plenty of prep space between.

As long as a second cook stays tight to a corner, the efficiency for multiple users is practical. As Darrell Waltrip would say, "Boogity, boogity, boogity – let's go racing, boys!"

269

Leslie Hart-Davidson

O ver the last decade, my buddy Mike has been on a culinary journey that leveled him up to a great cook and baker. One of the many treats he introduced to the Compound is this delightful fruit salsa. The fine chop of the ingredients made a hella-tasty appetizer (and an even better pancake topping the next morning).

2 kiwis, peeled and diced
2 Honeycrisp or other sturdy sweet apples, peeled, cored, and diced finely
8 oz raspberries, quartered
1 lb strawberries, topped and diced
2 tsp sugar
1 TB brown sugar
3 tsp fruit preserves (raspberry or strawberry)
10 flour tortillas (soft taco size)
Butter-flavored cooking spray
2 TB cinnamon sugar

Directions

In a large bowl, toss in the kiwis, apples, raspberries, strawberries, and fruit preserves. Mix thoroughly, then sprinkle on the white and brown sugars. Give it a good stir, then cover and chill in the refrigerator at least 15 minutes while you whip up the crisps.

Preheat oven to 350. Lay out five-ish tortillas on a large parchment-lined baking sheet and coat the top side with a generous dose of butter flavored cooking spray. Cut into chip-sized wedges (about 8 pieces per tortilla) and arrange in a single layer. Sprinkle with desired amount of cinnamon sugar and hit the wedges again with another spray to set the sprinkles. Bake for 8-10 minutes until crispy. Remove the parchment paper from the baking sheet to allow the wedges to cool and repeat with any remaining tortillas. Serve with the chilled fruit salsa.

Yields: 6-8 servings
Pairs with: a summer dinner.
Consideration: dice no bigger than pea size for proper consistency.

Just like summer tomatoes, fruit in season will tend to mush a bit, but will be crazy delicious

talc

Now that you have CRAP concepts under your belt, let's level up and give some quality time to functionality on a bigger scale.

When my clients do the deep dive into HGTV shows and demand that I replicate the stunning open concept, sleek finished, minimalist kitchen of their dreams featured so prominently on the remodeling shows, I take a deep breath and introduce them to TALC. No, not the powder; the second concept I created to help with kitchen design.

TALC is the acronym for four room-related sensory experiences: Texture, Acoustics, Lighting and Convection. While the goal of CRAP is visual, the purpose of TALC is physical. Feeling good and being safe in a space, especially a functional room like a kitchen, is critical to a successful design.

My clients who love the sleek open concept kitchens popular on HGTV are missing a key sensory experience when looking at those remodels. For example, kitchens of that style frequently have acoustical issues. The lack of walls in an open concept allows normal kitchen sounds to travel, meaning that a family member trying to watch tv in the adjoining room will be challenged while someone is clanking dishes. Another big issue is the convection pattern. Proper cooktop ventilation is based on the cubic footage of the entire room, meaning that a cute little hood vent will be ineffective in removing cooking odors. The adjoining living room furniture will smell like dinner for days after a big meal unless the convection is correctly sized.

Food is Love

Let's take a look at each of the four TALC elements using my remodeled farm kitchen to see how impactful they are in the overall design.

texture

acoustics

lighting

convection

TALC was first introduced in *It's Not Your Room, It's You,* Leslie's second interior design book that reflects on the relationships people have with their spaces.

273

Leslie Hart-Davidson

wipe-ability

Leather seating at the island closest to the stove was a specific choice: its wipeable upholstery is easy to clean and maintain.

de-fingerprint

The black stainless finish on the appliances is mostly fingerprint-resistant. I only occasionally obsess over cleaning it.

talc

texture

Texture is the experience of your body bits (fingers, hands, feet) touching surfaces in your kitchen. Surfaces include countertops, flooring, cabinet knobs, appliance handles, seating— anything that your body comes in direct contact with as you navigate your kitchen space.

When evaluating the texture of a room, it's important to ask yourself this question: how does this surface make me feel, and how easy will it be to clean and maintain?

easy-peasy clean up

The bar area with prep sink features a vintage wood top with a marine varnish finish that's a breeze to maintain. The slick top is easily cleaned to remove wine spills.

275

Leslie Hart-Davidson

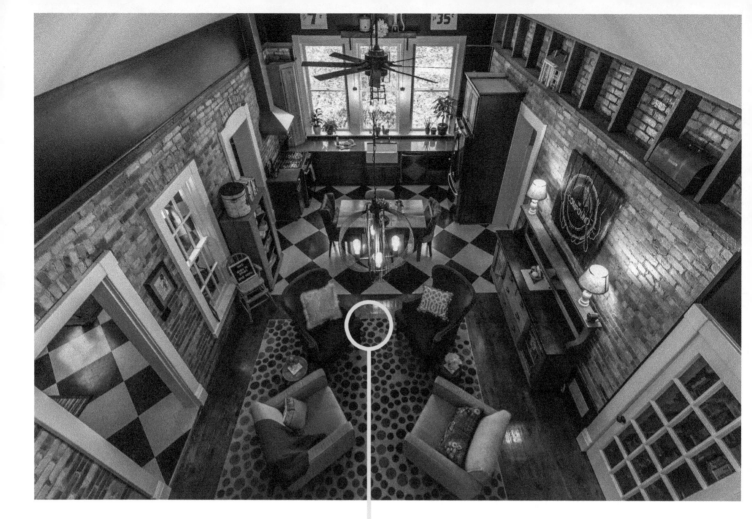

textile sound absorption

The volume of the combined kitchen and Starbucks area is massive, so sound would bounce like an endless game of Atari Pong without the help of textiles. The rug, upholstered furniture and mountain of toss pillows all absorb the sound like a champ so that Alexa will still respond from 20 feet away.

276

Food is Love

talc

acoustics

What? WHAT??? Acoustics is the experience of sound and how it bounces around in your space. Being able to hold a conversation without yelling (or on the flip side, without everyone hearing all that's said) is critical to the enjoyment and usability of the kitchen. When evaluating the acoustics of a room, it's important to ask yourself this T Mobile inspired question: "Can you hear me now?"

The danger of the insanely popular open concept layout is that the users of the space can hear everything from whispered conversations to pot clanking to spoons dropping in the sink. Fridge raiding at 3am just got a lot harder.

To combat the amplified echo from an open concept, it's important to layer as many textiles and art pieces as possible in the room. Upholstered seating, rugs, pillows, drapery, and canvas artwork will all minimize the sound bounce.

Leslie Hart-Davidson

ambient light

These sweet table lamps provide ambient lighting in the Starbucks area.

general light

This rectangular metal chandelier provides general lighting for the kitchen triangle.

Food is Love

lighting

GENERAL
AMBIENT
TASK

Lighting is the experience of being able to see your room and function properly in it when natural sunlight isn't available. There are three key levels of lighting for your kitchen: *general* (the first switch-you-flip layer), *task* (to concentrate on what's right in front of you), and *ambient* (bonus mood lighting that's usually on a dimmer).

Lighting isn't just functional. It can completely alter the way you FEEL in a space based on the quantity of lumens and quality of light being used.

task lighting

This funky llama lamp provides task lighting while chopping veggies next to the cooktop.

Leslie Hart-Davidson

QUANTITY

Too much lighting

An overabundance of high-lumen bulbs, especially in a downward configuration, can lead to uncomfortable feelings of interrogation. If innocuous questions at the dining table like "How was your day, dear?" make you feel like spewing a Colonel Jessup-style rant of "You want me on that wall! You need me on that wall!", you likely have too much lighting in your room.

Too little lighting

A lack of lighting in a kitchen can be depressing and dangerous. Poor task lighting can result in lost fingers while chopping broccoli (cue Dana Carvey). If you have already maxed out the lumens in your existing light fixtures, don't be afraid to add an actual table lamp to your kitchen counter. I promise you it's an enlightening experience. Heh.

QUALITY

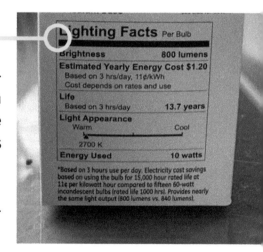

Wrong type

A poorly chosen light bulb can leave you feeling depressed and looking cyanotic. If you're trying to rock a goth lifestyle, knock yourself out. If not, check out the detail on the side of each lightbulb package that looks shockingly similar to an FDA food label.

The Kelvin rating will help you choose the proper quality of bulb to fit your need.

talc

lighting

Let's diagnose common lighting issues in a space by first learning about color temperature.

QUANTITY
QUALITY

Kelvin Scale

The "warm" side begins at 2700 K and the "cool" side ends at 6500 K. Warm lighting is like a candle or traditional incandescent bulb. It promotes a healthy skin glow and makes us feel warm and cozy. Cool lighting is like a clear, cloudless sky. The blueish cast to the light is terrible for makeup and can leave us feeling cold like a Dementor is floating nearby. Be mindful of what the package says when purchasing bulbs: Daylight=Dementor!

Leslie Hart-Davidson

ceiling fan

This monster ceiling fan is the proper scale to redirect air for the volume of space. Bonus: cats love watching the giant blades spin.

Tip: There's a nifty little switch located on the motor of your ceiling fan that reverses the direction of the fan blades to push the warm air at the ceiling back down in winter. Placing the fan on the lowest setting with the blades turning clockwise in the colder months will help your vaulted room feel much more comfortable.

exhaust fan

This commercial grade Z Line exhaust fan can suck up small pets and children along with cooking odors. The larger the volume of the space, the more cfm (cubic feet per minute) the fan needs to be effective.

Tip: Crank the exhaust fan. One drawback to open concept kitchen and living spaces is scent related: cooking odors have no respect for boundaries and will infiltrate every single inch of your home. Installing and actually *using* the exhaust fan above your cooktop is the best way to keep those pesky odors contained while removing the moisture, heat and smoke from the kitchen. Recirculating fans filter the cooking odors and return them directly to the room through the same unit. Vented exhaust fans are preferable because they suck the cooking odors from the kitchen and send them outside where they belong.

Food is Love

talc

convection

Convection as it applies to TALC principles is the circulation of air through a room, contributing to the comfort of both temperature and scent. A room might look beautiful, but if the air is an inappropriate temperature or the fan is too powerful, it won't be comfortable to use the room for long.

With the invention of forced convection from furnaces and air conditioning units starting in the 1930's, the comfort of a room is far more controllable. Home styles of today tend to push the boundaries of convection with massive vaulted ceilings and open concept kitchens, so let's examine common convection issues and how to address them. Being smart about airflow can make the space comfortable as well as beautiful.

Leslie Hart-Davidson

Spring and summer gatherings at Grandma Drennen's house were never complete without a big serving of Lemon Lush. This dish is straight-up late 1960's Betty Crocker gangster baking in the dessert world. Mrs. Draper called, ladies. She wants her Pyrex back.

1 ½ sticks butter
1 ½ C flour
1 C powdered sugar
1 C Cool Whip
2 - 3 ½ oz packages instant lemon pudding
2 ¾ C milk
1 8 oz tub Cool Whip
1 8 oz pkg cream cheese

Directions

Preheat the oven to 350 degrees. In a large bowl, mix the butter and flour. Press into the bottom of the Pyrex dish. Bake for 15 minutes, then allow to cool.

Grab another large bowl and mix up the powdered sugar, 1 cup of Cool Whip and cream cheese. When it's all nice and fluffy, spread it over the cooled crust.

In yet another bowl (or just keep using the same damn one that you rinse out), beat the two packages of instant pudding with milk for the length of time it takes a teenager to lose interest in new technology (about 2 to 3 minutes). Pour the electric-colored puddin' over the fluffy white layer and spread evenly with a rubber spatula. Finally, add the rest of the tub of Cool Whip and swirl it around until the layer is covered.

Refrigerate overnight for best results. If you don't have that much time, at least do your best Samuel L. Jackson impression and tell that bitch to chill for a few hours before serving.

What's Fonzie like, Yolanda? Cool. That's right.

Yields: 6 servings
Pairs with: a martini and a nod to Betty Draper.
Consideration: don't leave in the sun during picnics.

for extra special presentation, top with berries or citrus zest.

history of kitchens

Russel Morash is responsible for my career. Who is Russ, you ask? Oh, just the genius WGBH Boston producer/director who brilliantly birthed the twin genres of cooking and home improvement shows. Russ introduced Julia Child to the world in 1963 with *The French Chef* and worked with her for thirty years to help viewers love all things kitchen related. In 1979, Russ had an epiphany after hiring Norm Abram to remodel his own historical home and created *This Old House*, the first home renovation show whose episodes now number over one thousand.

As a foodie and a trained designer, I have immense respect for the knowledge that Russ Morash unleashed upon this world. Cooking and design have been good buddies since the dawn of time. Cooking spaces, whether rustic or refined, have a symbiotic relationship between efficiency and beauty. Archeological finds from some of the earliest cooking sites include exquisitely carved clay pots, yet the fanciest kitchens of today where we often don't cook still provide the space for us to gather for a meal like our ancestors did a thousand years ago. Let's take a look at the history of kitchens and how influences like marketing and television impacted its design.

"Cooking is one of the strongest ceremonies for life."

Laura Esquivel

"No one who cooks, cooks alone. Even at her most solitary, a cook in the kitchen is surrounded by generations of cooks past, the advice and menus of cooks present, the wisdom of cookbook writers."

Laurie Colwin

"My kitchen is a mystical place, a kind of temple for me. It is a place where the surfaces seem to have significance, where the sounds and odors carry meaning that transfers from the past and bridges to the future."

Pearl Bailey

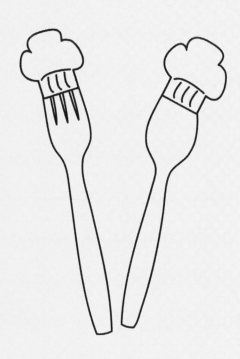

287

Leslie Hart-Davidson

Pre-Colonial Era

Indigenous peoples were brilliant, efficient cooks for their families and communities. Their agricultural game was strong, supplementing the fishing and hunting efforts to create meals that could be cooked over an open fire outside on a tripod, buried knee deep in an earthen pit, or in a row of individual fires inside a Longhouse like the Iriquois created. The Native communities fashioned beautiful, functional vessels from clay for slow cooking and frequently used stones from other fires to pop in crocks to cook stews. Then..... white people came.

1600-1700s

Dutch settlers and the next century of immigrants built homes with an open hearth and fireplace for cooking by hanging pots over the fire. Turnspit dogs were often trained to turn the roasting wheel in the large open fireplace to evenly cook meat (14/10 would reward with a nibble). Who did the cooking? Women in the family, hired help, and a headshaking number of enslaved workers.

1800s

Coal and iron mining made the first cast iron stove possible. The Oberlin Stove patented in 1834 was a game changer for American kitchens, allowing for more precise cooking with wood or coal fuel in a contained capacity instead of an open fire. Caroline Ingalls just loved her cast iron stove, but was crushed that Laura sold her horse to that bitch Nellie Olsen to pay for it.

288

Food is Love

1898

The industrial revolution's emphasis on functionality leaked over into the kitchen, and the super efficient Hoosier Cabinet was born. Invented by the Hoosier Cabinet Company in New Castle, IN, these independent pieces contained a ton of functionality for baking, cooking and storage and would make future Karens fight over them at antique malls 100+ years later.

1910

WWI spawned the creation of the United States Food Administration headed by pre-president Herbert Hoover. Hoover's efforts to ration food to feed the troops were successful with catchy programs like Meatless Mondays, Taco Tuesdays and Wheatless Wednesdays. Most homes by this point were connected to a municipal water system, so freestanding sinks became a THING.

1920s

Most American homes had a gas line, so stoves no longer needed wood fire tending. Hoosier Cabinets experienced the height of their popularity, setting up a path for both ergonomic efficiency and unrealistic expectations for women in the kitchen for generations to come.

Leslie Hart-Davidson

1930s

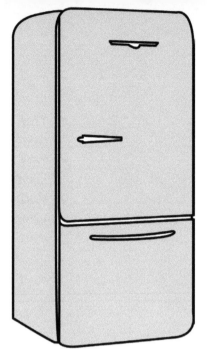

In the same way Edison promoted electric light installation and usage because he owned the power company, General Electric promoted the idea of leftovers to sell more fancy new electric refrigerators they manufactured. Other electric appliances completed the suite, leading to the birth of the first "fitted" kitchen with built-in cabinets and countertops.

1940s

Factories that produced weapons during the war pulled a brilliant switcheroo and began manufacturing steel kitchen cabinetry to outfit the boom of new construction. Post-war manufacturing technology played a big role in finishes like linoleum flooring and durable countertops for swoonworthy, efficient kitchens to console women who traded their Rosie the Riveter gigs for a June Cleaver role. "Thanks for your efforts in the factories, toots! Now go make me a turkey pot pie."

1950s

For the first time, kitchens started moving to the front of the house as a status symbol, often with pass-throughs to allow homemakers like Marion Cunningham to come up for air. Vibrant colors and styles in countertops and wallpaper along with cool new small appliances created the first "keeping up with the Joneses" look.

1960s

The space race and all things futuristic spawned kitchens inspired by The Jetsons. While 60's housewives didn't have the luxury of their own Rosie the Robot, at least they had a cool new dishwasher.

1970s

Dark wood cabinetry and mellower colors like harvest gold and avocado green for appliances and countertops were the hallmarks of the Brady Bunch era. Convenience foods and microwave ovens made an appearance to ease the burden of working women who were still responsible for all things domestic.

1980s

Gordon Gekko would feel right at home in the flashy, in-your-face look of the white plasticy and shiny brass kitchens built for entertaining and impressing neighbors. Celebrity chefs like Jacques Pépin and Martha Stewart encouraged home cooks to level up their cuisine from the tiny tv in the kitchen corner.

291

Leslie Hart-Davidson

1990s

Golden oak cabinetry became the go-to for all new construction kitchens which frequently featured a small island and a desk area that would quickly become the dumping ground for every member of the family (and a primary reason why Mommy needs a second glass of Cabernet every evening.) Higher-end kitchens of this time boasted hide-and-seek style appliances covered by matching cabinetry panels. "Heeeere fridge fridge fridge...."

2000s

HGTV created a market for flashy backsplash tile, stunning granite countertops and sleek white cabinetry that looked right at home on television. The Food Network did its level best to educate home cooks and raise the culinary bar on dinner ideas, but most Americans seemed to enjoy the *idea* of a pretty kitchen rather than the *use* of it.

2010 - present

Fully open floorplans create a stage effect for kitchens today, especially when the massive center island is a contrasting color from the main cabinetry. Luckily, the combo of easily cleanable quartz countertops, wicked smart appliances and grocery/meal delivery services make cooking far more accessible to everyone in the home.

Food is Love

Betty Crocker

Betty Crocker, the beloved mother of American cooking since the 1920's, *is a fictional character.* She was invented by the men who ran the company that would become General Mills in order to sell their shit. She first appeared on *The Betty Crocker Cooking School of the Air* in 1924 and was portrayed by multiple actresses through the decades on both radio and television. The Betty Crocker cookbook series has sold over 60 million copies.

293

Leslie Hart Davidson

My maternal Grandmother Thelma Mae Coffenberger Derr DeCamp was quite a character. Her first husband died young of polio in the 1950's, so she ran a tight ship while working full time at a high-end department store in downtown Springfield, Ohio. Goulash was quick, inexpensive and fed a bunch of folks, making it a go-to dinner. Thelma told me the recipe when I was newly married, so I tried it out. "It's kinda crunchy," I told Thelma when she called to ask how I had fared making it. "Well did you cook the pasta completely before you added it in?" she asked. "Um...before?" I replied. She sighed. "You don't put the raw shells in the pot, bottleass!" she replied. Lesson learned.

thelma's goulash

being called bottleass was a rite of passage.

1 lb 90% ground beef
1 28 oz can crushed tomatoes
2 14 oz cans diced tomatoes with juice
1 large yellow onion, diced
1 green bell pepper, diced
1 4 oz can mushrooms (pieces and stems)
1 TB minced garlic
2 tsp dried basil
2 TB evoo
2 tsp kosher salt
2 tsp black pepper
1 lb pasta shells
Grated parmesan cheese for topping

In a large pot, heat evoo on medium and sautée diced onions until translucent. Add the ground beef, occasionally mushing and chopping until the chunks are consistent in size and browned through.

Add garlic, basil, green pepper, and tomatoes. Give it a good stir and let it simmer hard for about 10ish minutes while you make the pasta.

Cook the pasta in a separate pan (thanks, Thelma) according to package directions. Drain and add directly to the pot o' goulash. Stir, check for seasonings and monkey with any other spices or heat you'd like to add. Serve with a sprinkling of grated parmesan cheese.

Food is Love

Yields: 6 servings
Pairs with: sweatpants and a strong will.
Consideration: rock macaroni if shells aren't your jam.

J im Hart had a spoiled feline companion named Buddy who was rescued as a grizzled old man from the dumpster area of Jim's workplace. Buddy was a snaggletooth boy, so Jim Hart lovingly cut up his bachelor leftovers into bite-size bits for the OG Grumpy Cat. One of Buddy's favorite meals was chicken wings with this gooey, tasty sauce. Humans think it's pretty damn tasty, too.

buddy's drummies
Everybody cooks for their cats, right?

3ish lbs chicken drummies or wings (24-30 pieces)
1 ½ C corn syrup
½ C Open Pit original barbeque sauce
¼ C Worcestershire sauce
¼ C apple cider vinegar
¼ C Dijon or stone ground mustard
1 TB chili powder
2 tsp garlic powder or chopped garlic
1 tsp paprika

Preheat the oven to 375 degrees. In a large bowl, dump in all of the goo and spices and give it a thorough whisk. Place the chicken bits in a Pyrex dish and douse the whole lot, tossing to cover. Pop in the oven and bake for 30 minutes, then flip the tasty clucky pieces and spoon the sauce over the lot. Cook for another 25ish minutes until GBD (golden, brown and delicious).

Yields: 6 servings
Pairs with: celery sticks and blue cheese.
Consideration: halve the recipe for a smaller crowd.

Buddy the cat

Don't forget the napkins!

Chicken Strip Send Off

Greg was specific in his instructions regarding his death: "I don't want a funeral. Cremate me. Put me in a niche as close to Mom as you can. I want my cat Annie's ashes in the niche with me." I took the last three instructions to heart and complied like a good sister. I liberally interpreted the "no funeral" wish, however. What I discovered during his illness is that Greg had a shitton of friends and co-workers who were all very concerned and wanted to mourn as a group. Instead of a funeral, I threw a memorial party. I wanted it to be as Greg-like as possible, so I was inspired by his favorite things: Chicken strips, ketchup, baked goods, Star Wars and humor. I booked a hotel banquet room and threw a party called "Greg Hart's Chicken Strip Sendoff." I had catering bring in chicken strips and gallons of ketchup for dipping. His fantastic coworkers at Pepsi brought in a gross of Schuler's brownies, and I custom made labels with my brother's face on them to cover 100 bottles of Heinz ketchup as party favors. The commemorative ketchups sat at a table flanked by 70" tall helium-filled Stormtrooper balloons and nostalgic poster-size pictures of my brother.

As is the custom in my family, I write eulogies. Funny eulogies, to be exact. I never intend disrespect for the dead, but humor is one of the only tools to successfully combat grief. I had an easy time coming up with the hilarious stories to tell at Greg's memorial, but I felt like I had a bigger opportunity to use his death, or his acceptance of his own mortality to be exact, to teach others about the beauty of his non-subjunctive life. Without knowing it, he fully participated in Give.

During my combined 18,000 mile journey to help Greg, I listened to a ridonkulous amount of podcasts and TED Talks. One TEDx talk resonated completely as I marveled at Greg's ability to stay positive and forward-thinking about his care. Phuc Tran, a Classicist, gave a talk in 2012 called "Grammar, Identity, and the Dark Side of the Subjunctive." In the talk, Tran explains that in the language of his Vietnamese parents, the subjunctive tense does not exist. There is no option for considering possibilities of what did not happen or what hasn't yet happened. There were only two tenses that existed: the indicative (the current reality) and the imperative (your next move). I drew many parallels between what Greg had taught me during his care and what Phuc Tran taught me about the language.

At the memorial, I offered the idea of Greg's intentional language choice to the audience in Star Wars terms. "Darth Vader and the Sith Lords generally speak in the subjunctive," I began. "'If you only knew the power of the dark side,'" Vader said to Luke. "Yoda," I continued, "speaks only in the imperative and indicative. 'Do or do not. There is no try.'" I ended the memorial with a request that everyone live a little more indicatively to honor Greg. "Take a commemorative ketchup with you and smile every time you use the bottle," I reminded them. "And may the force be with you."

chicken strip send off

rocket slide

My knuckles were white. The metal was hot. My breathing was shallow. I opened my eyes and screamed for my brother as I sat at the top of the Rocket Slide at Reid Park. My four-year-old smartass mouth got me into this situation when Greg dared me to go down the massive slide. "I bet you're too chicken to do it!" he taunted, so I got in the long line and ascended the walkway to the top. Greg stood below, watching my progress. When I finally reached the top and took in the view, I was overwhelmed. Greg recognized the terror on my face and claimed victory over my chickenshittedness, but quickly realized that I wasn't coming down on my own. His expression changed from celebration to exasperation in a heartbeat as he took off for the line and pushed his way past everyone to get to me.

"Aw c'mon, whydja let that little baby up here? You're ruining our fun!" the bratty boy in a dirty Incredible Hulk T-shirt behind me yelled at my brother. "Lay off!" he replied, then nudged the mouthy kid aside to join me at the top. Greg grabbed me by my armpits and slid his legs beneath mine so that I ended up on his lap. My white knuckles were still firmly attached to the metal rails, however. "Okay, let go!" he said. "NO!" I yelled, still frightened. "You have to let go now. It's time. People are waiting for you." "I'm scared," I told him. "I've got you," Greg said. "So just let go."

I released my death grip on the metal and watched as Greg's Converse shoes scooched us forward. The rush of the wind was thrilling as we slid down. Wait — did I actually enjoy the slide? I did! The momentary fright was absolutely worth it. I smiled up at Greg for rescuing me and showing me how to be brave once again. He shook his head and went back to his friends.

Thirty years later, Greg and I are together again to experience another adrenaline rush. The Banshee is a new badass roller coaster at Kings Island and we waited in line a solid hour for the thrill. As the clicks grew louder and faster towards the top of the hill, my brother eyed my white knuckles clenching the warm metal harness grips and heard my shallow breathing. "Hey!" he yelled over the clicking. "Don't hang on. The fall is better if you just let go!" "NO!" I reply, shaking my head as we teeter at the top. "Listen to me!" Greg yelled while kicking his sneaker against my foot. "Just let go!" His sneaker takes me back to the Rocket Slide and I dutifully removed my death grip. With one giant deep breath, I raised my arms over my head and prepared for the first hill. The rush is AMAZEBALLS. Like Rocket-Slide-times-a-bazillion amazeballs. We sped through the loops and hills and turns, and arrived with a jerk at the station. I looked over at Greg and smiled through the adrenaline rush. "Again!" I yelled at him. "Told you so," he replied, shaking his head.

Today, my knuckles are white as I hold the warm metal bed rail and look at my big brother. My breathing is shallow, but his is labored. The five months of battle have taken their toll on his body. Greg's wishes a few days ago were crystal clear: he's tired and done. "Keep me warm and out of pain," he rasped. I tuck the blanket around his 80lb frame and adjust his pillow again. I lean down and channel the lessons from the Rocket Slide and the roller coaster. "You have to let go now," I tell him. "It's time. People are waiting for you." Greg passed away peacefully this morning. I want to thank everyone for the kindness and prayers during these many months of struggle. I'm honored to have been able to care for him. These stories have helped me process so much of the grief and channel it into something useful and entertaining. I hope you've enjoyed them.

My big brother Greg was known for three things: his kindness, ripped physique, and single-mindedness when it came to restaurant orders. Over the years of dining out with him, I consistently heard "Yeah, I'll take the chicken fingers basket." I found a recipe using crushed potato chips as a coating to make them at home. Whenever I'm missing Greg, I whip out the strips and a big splat of ketchup.

1 10 oz bag bbq or regular flavor potato chips, crushed
3 eggs, beaten
1 ½ lbs chicken tender strips (about 12 will fit on a large baking sheet)
Sauces for dipping

Directions

Preheat the oven to 400 degrees. In a medium bowl, crack the eggs and whippy dippy. Place the chips in a gallon storage bag, press out the air, and flatten them with the vengeance of the wronged. Put the eggs and chips in two different pans for the purpose of dredging and prepare a baking sheet lined with parchment or non-stick foil.

Lay out a sheet of waxed paper about 2' long on a flat counter. Place the chicken tenders close together, then cover with another piece of waxed paper. Pound the tenders to a uniform 1/4" ish thickness using a paillard mallet (thanks, Martha Stewart) or a rolling pin.

With a fork, dip a piece of pounded chicken in the beaten egg, then plop in the crushed chips. Flick some chips over the top of the chicken with a fork, then press the top to adhere the chips. Place the dredged chicken piece on the lined baking sheet and repeat for all of the other pieces.

Bake for 10-12 minutes until no longer pink in the center. Serve with dipping sauce of your choice.

Yields: 6 servings
Pairs with: all the sauces and maybe a veg.
Consideration: have fun with multiple chip flavors.

You can also make nuggets by cutting each strip in fourths.

Main Dishes

Side Dishes

Appetizers

Desserts

Party Fare

About the Author

Upon meeting LHD, prepare to state you super power and level up. She may be an accomplished interior designer, national speaker on design and space functionality, guest lecturer on interior design entrepreneurship, successful author and bad-ass foodie who knows her way around the kitchen. But more importantly, she's that mentor that leads you to find the best version of yourself, without you even knowing it's happening. All of a sudden you are more confident, more capable and can leap buildings in a single bound. Maybe not that last one, but close. Whatever your super power is, she will find it and amplify it.

Like in her two previous books, *Remodeling Your House Without Killing Your Spouse* and *It's Not Your Room, It's You*, Leslie will give you the tools, motivation and permission to find your own path to success. Pulling from her real estate flipper-parents upbringing, formal education at Bowling Green State University (class of '94), and decades of hands-on retail management experience, you'll feel more comfortable in the kitchen, regardless of what side of the stove you are on.

Follow her on social media, enjoy the heck out of *Food is Love* and ask her over for dinner. You won't regret it. After almost 20 years of enjoying meals at the Compound and watching her use her super powers to give to others, I certainly don't regret one second.

-Kitten

CPSIA information can be obtained
at www.ICGtesting.com
Printed in the USA
LVHW070300280521
688743LV00002B/8